The Shakespeare Handbooks   General Editor: John Russell Brown

Much Ado About Nothing shows the violence of desire as well as its drive towards creative plotting or matchmaking. In this Handbook, Alison Findlay examines the play's comic and tragic potential in the theatre and its attempts to harmonise love and war, attraction and repulsion. The book:

• explores the play's resonance in early performances with reference to the crisis over fast-changing fashions, gendered notions of honour and the changing personnel of Shakespeare's company
• analyses the play from a performance point of view scene by scene, considering the interactions between spectators and actors
• surveys key productions and films, including the recently rediscovered television film of Zeffirelli's 1965 National Theatre Production, Barry Jackson's radical modernist production of 1919 and Kenneth Branagh's film version
• outlines the play's critical history from the eighteenth century to the present day, with a focus on contemporary concerns such as genre hybridity, sources and intertexts and the instability of signs and appearances.

Alison Findlay is Professor of Renaissance Drama and Director of the Shakespeare Programme at Lancaster University. Her publications include *Playing Spaces in Early Women's Drama* (2006) and *Women in Shakespeare* (2010).

The Shakespeare Handbooks are student-friendly introductory guides which offer a new approach to understanding Shakespeare's plays in performance. The commentary at the heart of each volume explores the play's theatrical potential, providing an experience as close as possible to seeing it in the theatre. The Handbooks also offer contextual documents, a brief history of the text and its first performances, case studies of key productions, a wide sampling of critical opinion and guidance on further reading. Ideal for students and teachers of Literature and Theatre, as well as actors and directors, the overall aim is to help a reader reach an independent and well-informed view of each play by imagining how it might be performed on stage.

THE SHAKESPEARE HANDBOOKS

Series Editor: John Russell Brown

PUBLISHED

The Shakespeare Handbooks

Much Ado About Nothing

Alison Findlay

palgrave
macmillan

First published 2011 by
PALGRAVE MACMILLAN

Palgrave Macmillan in the UK is an imprint of Macmillan Publishers Limited,
registered in England, company number 785998, of Houndmills, Basingstoke,
Hampshire RG21 6XS.

Palgrave Macmillan in the US is a division of St Martin's Press LLC,
175 Fifth Avenue, New York, NY 10010.

Palgrave Macmillan is the global academic imprint of the above companies
and has companies and representatives throughout the world.

Palgrave® and Macmillan® are registered trademarks in the United States,
the United Kingdom, Europe and other countries.

ISBN 978–0–230–22260–1 hardback
ISBN 978–0–230–22261–8 paperback

This book is printed on paper suitable for recycling and made from fully
managed and sustained forest sources. Logging, pulping and manufacturing
processes are expected to conform to the environmental regulations of the
country of origin.

A catalogue record for this book is available from the British Library.

A catalog record for this book is available from the Library of Congress.

10   9   8   7   6   5   4   3   2   1
20 19 18 17 16 15 14 13 12 11

Printed and bound in China

To David, Robert and Eleanor, with love

Note: All references to *Much Ado About Nothing* are to McEachern, Claire, ed. *Much Ado About Nothing*, Arden Third Series (Cengage Learning, 2005).

All references to other plays by Shakespeare are to texts in *The Riverside Shakespeare*, second edition (Houghton Mifflin Company, 1997).

All biblical references are to the King James Bible (1611).

Contents

General Editor's Preface

The Shakespeare Handbooks provide an innovative way of studying the plays in performance. The commentaries, which are their core feature, enable a reader to envisage the words of a text unfurling in performance, involving actions and meanings not readily perceived except in rehearsal or performance. The aim is to present the plays in the environment for which they were written and to offer an experience as close as possible to an audience's progressive experience of a production.

While each book has the same range of contents, their authors have been encouraged to shape them according to their own critical and scholarly understanding and their first-hand experience of theatre practice. The various chapters are designed to complement the commentaries: the cultural context of each play is presented together with quotations from original sources; the authority of its text or texts is considered with what is known of the earliest performances; key performances and productions of its subsequent stage history are both described and compared; an account is given of influential criticism of the play and the more significant is quoted extensively. The aim in all this has been to help readers to develop their own informed and imaginative view of a play in ways that supplement the provision of standard editions and are more user-friendly than detailed stage histories or collections of criticism from diverse sources.

Further volumes are in preparation so that, within a few years, the Shakespeare Handbooks will be available for all the plays that are frequently performed and studied.

John Russell Brown

Acknowledgements

I wish to thank the staff of Lancaster University Library, the Shakespeare Centre Library, Gavin Clarke at the National Theatre Archive and Cherie Gladstone and staff at Birmingham Central Library for their help in locating materials referred to in this book. My thanks are also due to Kathleen Dickson at the British Film Institute for arranging immediate access to the recently recovered 1967 television recording of the National Theatre production of *Much Ado*. John Russell Brown has been a wonderfully perceptive general editor, drawing on his own experience of directing and watching the play to offer helpful observations. Claire McEachern has also helped me by commenting on a draft of the first part of the Commentary. I wish to thank both of them. I owe thanks, too, to Sonya Barker at Palgrave Macmillan who has skilfully transferred my manuscript into print. The copy editor has picked up errors which I have been able to correct; any which remain are my own. Finally, I thank David, Robert and Eleanor for their loving support, their sharp observation of film versions and, perhaps most importantly, for reminding me how funny *Much Ado About Nothing* is.

1 *The Text and Early Performances*

The first mention of '*The comedie of much A dooe about nothinge*' as 'A *booke*', was in a note, dated 4 August 1600, on the fly-leaf of a volume of the Stationer's Register, where it was formally entered on 23 August, and then appeared later that year in a quarto text (a book made up of sheets of paper folded twice to provide 4 leaves or 8 pages). The title page announced it as:

Much adoe about
Nothing
As it hath been sundrie times publikely
acted by the right honourable, the Lord
Chamberlaine his servants.
Written by William Shakespeare.

Further details on the title page informed the first readers that the play was printed in 1600 by Valentine Simmes for Andrew Wise (who also published quartos of *Richard III*) and William Aspley, who was later involved, though not as a very active partner, in the publishing of the First Folio of Shakespeare's plays, due to his ownership of the rights in *Much Ado* and *Henry IV Part 2 (2 HIV)* (also printed by Simmes). The published quarto would have cost about 6d (Murphy, 2003, 30), the equivalent of an expensive seat at the Curtain, which was probably the first theatre in which *Much Ado* had '*been sundrie times* publikely acted', as the title page advertises. When the Lord Chamberlain's Men opened the Globe Theatre in summer 1599, *Much Ado* may have still been part of the active repertory alongside newer plays such as *Julius Caesar*, *As You Like It* and *Henry V*. The earliest performances of *Much Ado* probably date from after 7 September 1598 since it is absent from Francis Meres's list of Shakespearean plays in his book *Palladis Tamia: Wits*

Treasury (1598) which was listed in the Stationers' Register on this day. *Much Ado* was probably completed and brought into the repertoire late in 1598 or early in 1599.

At least one of the parts had to be reassigned in the processes of composition, rehearsal or early performance. Will Kemp, who was famous for his clowning roles, and is named in the speech prefixes for Dogberry in Act IV scene ii, left the Lord Chamberlain's Men's theatre company sometime before 11 February (when he started a 'nine days' wonder' of dancing from London to Norwich). The quarto attributes Dogberry's opening line to 'Keeper', his second to 'Andrew' and thereafter to 'Kemp', while Verges' lines are prefixed 'Cowley' so we know that Richard Cowley (an actor hired by the Chamberlain's Men), played this role. Kemp's place as the lead comic actor was taken over by Robert Armin, who was to become a writer of plays and verse in his own right. Armin developed the role of the Shakespearean fool as a witty wordsmith in Touchstone in *As You Like It*, Feste in *Twelfth Night* and the King Lear's Fool, which were written for him. The role of Dogberry, who is famous for his malapropisms, seems to mark the shift between Kemp and Armin's styles of clowning. Armin's frustrations at having been 'writ down an ass' (V.i.86), by having to take up a role written for Kemp (whose previous credits included Bottom), may have added an extra layer of comedy to Dogberry's wild protestations. The line certainly seemed to have significance for Armin because in the dedication of his jest book *The Italian Tailor and His Boy* (1609), he appeals to the Lady Elizabeth Fitzwater recalling his role as one 'who hath been writ downe for an Asse in his time, & pleades under *forma pauperis* in it still, not-withstanding his Constableship and Office' (Armin, 1609, sig. A3).

The 'writ downe' form of *Much Ado About Nothing* in the early texts is crucial in preserving the play, but even at this stage, where editorial interventions are minimal, it shapes knowledge differently to a performance. The role of Don John is a case in point as Alan Galey has argued. In the spoken script he is simply introduced as the Prince's brother who has been in rebellion against Don Pedro but is now reconciled to him. In the quarto and Folio texts, speech prefixes and stage directions provide the extra information that he is a bastard (and '*dumb John*' in the quarto, sig. B4, if this is not a mistake for Don). He is not named bastard in the spoken dialogue until Act IV scene i when Hero is accused of the same illegitimate sexual activity from which he was born. An unknowing audience can thus appreciate the moment of revelation in performance on stage or screen. Once he has been writ down a bastard in a script, however, readers cannot escape the significance of that label and its associations. Don John thus presents something of a textual crux for editors. If, following an editorial tradition tracing back to the first quarto, 'he is a series of graphic marks on the printed page, then he is a bastard from his first entrance'. If, however, the editor prioritises performance as the origin of the play's meaning, 'he is an effect of transcribed stage dialogue, his own and that of other characters' and so 'he is not a bastard until the precise moment when his crime is suspected' (Galey, 2004, 21).

Inconsistencies in the quarto text of *Much Ado* suggest that it was based on Shakespeare's authorial papers rather than a working theatre script. W.W. Greg commented: 'If ever there was a text printed from foul papers that still needed a good deal of correction to fit them for use in the theatre it is Q' (Greg, 1955, 279). For example, Margaret and Ursula are missing from the stage directions for Act II scene i and Conrade, Borachio and members of the Watch are not included in the entry for the examination scene Act IV scene ii. In the Watch's first appearance at Act III scene iii, which of the lines assigned to the Watch should be spoken by Seacoal, as chief watchman, is muddled by the confusion of the speech prefix 2 *Watch* (the second watchman to speak) for him at the beginning of the scene and 1 *Watch* (as the chief watchman) later (Wells, 1980). The stage directions for Leonato's entrances in Acts I and II include '*Innogen his wife*' and '*his wife*', a character who never speaks in either scene and has no more substance than the ghost of an idea in the early stages of composition. To include a mother for Hero who said nothing during the courtship, betrothal and broken wedding scenes would certainly place heavy-handed emphasis on the conventional silencing of women in early modern England, but this is not a realistic production choice for most theatre companies, including the Lord Chamberlain's Men. Other 'ghost' members of Leonato's household are '*a kinsman*' who enters at the beginning of Act II scene i and a son of Antonio who is mentioned in the second scene as a provider of music (I.ii.1–2). Balthasar is the character who sings in Act II scene iii and is asked to provide music at Hero's chamber (II.iii.86–87), but again the quarto text is unclear since it gives two separate entries for music: one at line 34 when Don Pedro, Claudio and Leonato enter '*with musicke*'; and the second six lines later which reads '*Enter Balthasar with musicke*'. This problem is resolved in the Folio text.

The text of *Much Ado* included in the First Folio of 1623 (much more expensively priced at about £1; the equivalent of 44 loaves of bread) appears to have been printed from a copy of the 1600 quarto annotated with some changes and corrections, but no longer extant. Kemp's ghostly presence still haunts the Folio text in the speech prefixes for Act IV scene ii, which have not been corrected. Some annotations do suggest details of performance practice. The name of '*Iacke Wilson*' is added to the stage direction opening Act II scene iii, indicating this was the singer cast to play Balthasar and the second entry for Balthasar and music is removed. Wilson was apprenticed to John Heminge in 1611, so may have made his debut as Balthasar at performances of *Much Ado* at Court in 1612–13. He went on to write songs for the King's Men and became a City Wait from 1622, a lutenist at Court in 1635 and, finally, a professor of music at Oxford in 1656. References to God are taken out from Act IV scene ii, probably as a result of censorship on religious grounds. Also missing is part of Don Pedro's critique of Benedick's new fashion 'in the shape of two countries at once, as, a German from the waist downward, all slops, and a Spaniard from the hip upward, no doublet' (III.ii.33–35). These lines were probably cut because they would have been undiplomatic at the performance given for the Court's Christmas revels in 1612–13. Prince Frederick, the Elector Palatine, was in Court, about to celebrate his marriage to Princess Elizabeth, the daughter of James I and Anna of Denmark. The play's comic treatment of courtship, its promotion of love succeeding war and its references to Sicilian gardens and festivities would have made a warm interlude to the wintry Court, which was in mourning for the death of Prince Henry, heir to the throne. The masked ball of Act II scene i would have mimicked the usual court practices of masking and dancing at Whitehall. Quite how appropriate the dramatisation of a broken wedding day would have been for an apprehensive bride-to-be is more questionable. Nevertheless, the play is included in both lists of plays for which John Heminge was paid by the Lord Chamberlain's office on 20 May 1613 for 'presenting before the Princess highnes the Lady Elizabeth and the Prince Pallatyne Elector' so it probably had a repeat performance. It is listed once as '*Much Adoe abowte nothinge*' and in the second list as '*Benedicte and Betteris*' (Malone Society, 1962, 55–56). Charles I, who would have seen these court performances, apparently wrote the names against the title of the play in his copy of the 1632 second edition of the Folio (Furness, 1899, xxii and 6).

Such re-titlings indicate the tendency, from the early 17th century, to prioritise the Beatrice-Benedick rather than the Hero-Claudio plot. Leonard Digges's 1640 edition of Shakespeare's poems alludes to both characters as a draw for audiences, suggesting that *Much Ado* enjoyed revivals in the public theatre:

> ... let but *Beatrice*
> And *Benedicke* be seene, loe in a trice
> The Cockpit[,] Galleries, Boxes, all are full.

(Digges, 1640, sig. A4)

Margaret Cavendish too listed '*Bettrice*' among Shakespeare's female characters that made one think 'he had been Metamorphosed from a Man to a Woman', in order to draw them so well (Thompson and Roberts, 1997, 13). Beatrice and Benedick's 'merry war' of words in the play makes them prototypes of the witty couple, a pairing that became a characteristic feature of the comedy of manners in post-Restoration drama. They thus represent one example of continuity between drama dating from before the English Civil Wars and that which followed. After the Restoration in 1660, Charles II licensed two theatre companies and *Much Ado* was assigned to the Duke's Company managed by Sir William D'Avenant. In spite of the increasing popularity of comedies featuring witty couples, late-17th century attitudes to Shakespeare's texts were to reform them in accordance with current tastes. D'Avenant spliced together the war of wit from the Beatrice and Benedick plot of *Much Ado* with a rewritten, more sentimental version of the main plot in *Measure for Measure*. In the new play *The Law Against Lovers* (1662), Beatrice, far from being an orphan, was recast as an heiress and ward to the Duke while Benedick was the brother of Angelo. Beatrice's exchange with the messenger, setting up the 'merry war', is transposed (D'Avenant, 1673, 274–75) but the first 'skirmish of wit' between the couple is supplemented by Beatrice's young sister, Viola, flirting with Benedick (276–77). Beatrice asks Benedick to help rescue her cousin, Julietta, by stealing Angelo's seal ring and forging a warrant for Claudio and Julietta's release, to which he agrees. In the final scene Beatrice jokes against marriage, telling Benedick 'Plays that end so begin to be / Out of fashion', but Benedick reminds her that 'a bauld Dramatick Poet / Of the next Cloister' (an allusion to the Friar and perhaps to Shakespeare) has advised Juliet 'to end her Tragy-Comedy / With Hymen the old way' (326). The Duke finally commands Beatrice and Benedick to 'joyful triumphs of a nuptial peace', in spite of Beatrice's comic protest that they will quarrel again (328).

The publication of Rowe's edition of Shakespeare in 1709, with a picture of the church scene as frontispiece, brought the full text of the play back into print and it was restored to the theatre in productions at Lincoln's Inn Fields in 1721 and in 1737 at Covent Garden. In addition to revivals in 1737, 1739 and 1746, it was also the subject of another adaptation, *The Universal Passion* (1737), by James Miller. The Hero-Claudio plot and elements from Molière's *La Princesse D'Elide* were put together in the romance of Lucilia and Bellario. Lucilia is a much more mature, spirited heroine than Hero, claiming, like Beatrice, that she has a 'natural Aversion to Marriage' so that death and a husband are the same to her (Miller, 1969, 9). She is wary of Bellario's court-ship, protesting 'Men only pretend to be our Slaves the present Hour, in order to be real Tyrants to us for the future' (8). The cross wooing of the masked ball is transferred to the women in this play, where Bellario declares his love for Liberia (21–22) and Lucilia is obliged to plead with her and with her father to prevent the match. Liberia, in the Don Pedro role, says 'my dear Child, I'll not steal thy Bird's Nest from thee' (26). More rivalry between the two is implied when Delia compares Lucilia's wedding gown to the grander fashion of Liberia's dress (49), whereas in Shakespeare's text, Margaret compares Hero's gown to the Duchess of Milan's.

The rivalry between characters offers ample opportunity for Byron, the Don John of this version, to plot. He adapts Edmund's sentiment to deride his brother, saying 'I was born in the pure State of Nature, he in the stale Marriage Bed' (15–16). The darker element of the wedding is already hinted at when the bride Lucilia states 'I'm now prepar'd to be a made a Sacrifice' (51). In the wedding scene, Bellario enters in 'Fun'ral Garb' which, as Gratiano points out 'suits but ill the Splendor of our Court' and 'its Pomp to grace your Nuptials'. Bellario darkly points out: 'My Lord, the Nuptial and the Fun'ral Rites / Are sometimes not so different in their Nature' (53). This is all we see of a funeral in *The Universal Passion*, which has no mourning scene for

Bellario to repent. Instead he is given an amalgamation of Romeo's mourning for Juliet and the praise of Cordelia's blessed, pearl-like tears as she wrings her hands (65). Bellario refuses the second match as impossible, asking for 'any other Chastisement'; his shock giving expression to spectators' uneasiness surrounding this part of Shakespeare's plot:

> But what! To wed another! hold, my Heart,
> Now dear Lucilia's lost – to wed another!
> Impossible; my Soul starts back with Horror,
> And Nature shudders at the very Sound.

(64)

Lucilia, who shares some of Beatrice's pride and self-declared aversion to marriage, gives voice to her unwarranted sense of injury in the church scene:

> Have I for this, ungrateful as thou art,
> When love of Freedom struggled in my Breast,
> And Nature prompted me to live a Virgin,
> Broke all those Vows to be thus basely treated;
> To have my Fame, unspotted 'till this Moment,
> Be sully'd, injur'd, ruin'd thus by thee.
> I need no Dagger's Point, – burst, burst, my Heart.

(55)

Like Hero, she collapses and disappears from the stage until her name is cleared. When Bellario is persuaded to take a second bride on trust 'with all her Imperfections' (69), and Lucilia is restored, she objects ('Hold, hold, my Lord'), not willing to accept him. She gives voice to the questions raised about what possible good reason she should have to trust him again:

> You may again bring Wretchedness upon me;
> And after I have once escap'd the Wreck,
> Why should I prove the boisterous Main again?

(70)

No answer is given to these valid points. Lucilia does not speak again; her hand is joined to Bellario's without any verbal consent on her part.

The more vigorous characterisation of Lucilia makes the figure of Liberia less of a contrast to the romantic heroine than in Shakespeare's play. Liberia adopts many of Beatrice's lines and some of Benedick's qualities, declaring 'my Heart's a sound as a Bell' (9). It is hinted, however, that she is feeling left out of the wedding preparations, protesting too much that because 'I abhor the Thoughts of committing Matrimony so much, that I can't endure the Preparation even for another'. Liberia goes on to sing Balthasar's song with an amended first line: '*Sigh no more, Virgins, sigh no more, / Men were deceivers ever;*' (39). She and Protheus fall victim to the plots of their friends in overhearing scenes which follow Shakespeare's quite closely but use the couple's reactions to marriage to balance the demands and appeal of romantic comedy against the supposedly more fashionable, worldly rejection of it. Liberia maintains an anti-romantic tenor right to the end of the play. Just before dancing with Protheus, she sings against '*Such Bondage*' as marriage will bring (73–74). Protheus ends the play proper by declaring that they should be an example to the world that honourable wedlock 'May, spite of Rallery, once more come in Fashion' and 'LOVE still reign the UNIVERSAL PASSION' (76). In case this view should prove too sentimental for spectators, Mrs Clive, who played Liberia, counters it with a distinctly anti-romantic epilogue saying the author is 'Non compos mentis' for ending the play in this way (77). As an adaptation, *The Universal Passion* thus provides quite a trenchant critique of Shakespeare's original, giving Lucilia much more of a voice than Hero, and raising questions about the romantic plot that have preoccupied critical writing.

2   *Commentary*

Act I

Act I, scene i

The play opens on a threshold, spatially and metaphorically, as Leonato interrogates the messenger, with the women of his family attending. This is also a temporal threshold: the transition between war and peacetime, violence and love. The messenger's news is materialised onstage by the letter that Leonato carries and refers to; as a physical object that epitomises meaning in transit, it effectively heralds the anticipation of imminent movement and change that characterises the atmosphere of these opening lines. The early texts do not specify where this scene takes place but it must be somewhere near the entrance to Leonato's house since Don Pedro says to him 'are you come to meet your trouble' (I.i.91–92) and Antonio later claims that Don Pedro and Claudio's conversation which ends the scene takes place in Leonato's orchard. Borachio claims he has overheard them while he was airing a musty room. In an Elizabethan staging he could have literally overheard by entering at the gallery above the stage. A large entrance which can be left open is required so that characters can begin the process of 'noting' or overhearing. A physical setting near the threshold of Leonato's house would reinforce the sense of liminality, a time and place of transition.

1–27   Hero and Beatrice's interests in Claudio and Benedick must add tension to Leonato's question 'How many gentlemen have you lost in this action?' (I.i.5–6), and the answer may be followed by some non-verbal expressions of relief or pleasure on the part of the women and Leonato. A production may choose to realise the quarto's stage direction for the entrance of Innogen, the wife of Leonato, who does

9

not speak in the play at all. If she does occupy stage space as a silent bodily presence in this scene, she makes a dramatic contrast to the outspoken Beatrice. Leonato's dialogue about Claudio's military success could be delivered as intended for Hero's benefit, implying that she and Claudio have had a prior history before he went to war (see I.i.280). If so, it should provoke signs of interest from Hero and her confidante Beatrice.

The detail about Claudio's uncle weeping with joy at the news is superfluous and irrelevant in plot terms but may serve to draw attention to a non-verbal reaction on Hero's part, if she weeps with relief (thus setting up a bond of sympathy with Claudio to reinforce their sparse dialogue and suggest a romantic tenderness). Any hints of a prior relationship between them complicate Leonato's alacrity to marry her off to Don Pedro when he hears the rumour of the Prince's intention to woo her at the ball (I.ii.10–12).

28–90 Beatrice has not yet heard about Benedick, even though he is presumably a man 'of name' and thus still alive. Her interest in him provokes the question 'Is Signor Mountanto returned from the wars or no?' (I.i.28–29), where her jokey name for him telegraphs the combination of desire and aggression that characterises her feelings for him. Hero recognises who Beatrice means as Beatrice knows she will, and provides Benedick's name. Beatrice's brilliant display of rhetorical skill in dialogue with the messenger makes it clear that the domestic, romantic arena will still deploy the tactics of aggression and strategy and the violence typical of the battlefield. Her delivery should be quick, her tone sharp but ostentatiously playful, running rings round the messenger. Leonato refers to the relationship between Beatrice and Benedick as a 'merry war' and 'skirmish of wit' (I.i.58–59); her rhetorical fencing with the messenger is the verbal equivalent of a warm-up: preparing both Beatrice and the audience for the duel of wit that is staged 50 lines later. The messenger's line 'Don Pedro is approached' may be cued by a sound effect or by the entrance of the soldiers. It should provoke a non-verbal reaction from Leonato and his family, as they arrange themselves (perhaps hurriedly) to formally receive Don Pedro and his companions. Hero as the hostess is probably placed to the fore with her father (unless the production also chooses to stage Innogen, who would occupy this prime position next to Leonato). Beatrice is slightly behind or to one side as a dependent within the household.

This would give her time to observe Benedick unnoticed until she makes her pointed entry into the dialogue (I.i.110).

91 Enter DON PEDRO, CLAUDIO, BENEDICK, BALTHASAR *and* [DON] JOHN *the bastard* The entrance of Don Pedro and his followers to the stage and to Leonato's household kinaesthetically marks the transition from war to peace, hostile aggression to romance, which is typical of the comic genre. The soldiers' homecoming may be highlighted non-verbally by the removal of weapons or military clothing: jackets, spurs, or perhaps even boots in a less formal meeting. Leonato's welcome may be extended with drinks, bowls and cloths for washing, a ritual preparation for entering the house of festivity and romance. The quarto lists Balthasar the musician as one of the entrants, so the soldiers' arrival may be heralded by a trumpet flourish. Don John, the bastard brother of Don Pedro is also listed but is not addressed and does not speak until some 55 lines later. One production choice is to give him a separate entrance before Leonato greets him (I.i.147), but such a choice misses an important opportunity to establish him as a silent, malcontented presence on the stage (a theatrical equivalent to Hamlet in Act I scene ii at the court of Elsinore). His bastardy is not mentioned until Act IV scene i, although it could be announced silently by the use of a band sinister, the heraldic symbol of illegitimacy, on his coat of arms (see above pp. 2–3 on the consequences of labelling Don John a bastard). For early modern spectators, the bar sinister showing his bastard status would have signalled the limits of his reacceptance into his brother's household. His melancholy may be telegraphed by dark clothing typical of the malcontent. Since his rebellion against Don Pedro has recently been quashed, he is probably unarmed, and can either by hustled on as a trophy or included as a social inferior who is now 'reconciled' (I.i.148) to Don Pedro. Although not marked in the quarto stage directions, his attendants Conrade and possibly Borachio probably make an entrance here too, thus mirroring Don Pedro's cohort of Claudio and Benedick.

91–110 As the socially superior figure, Don Pedro speaks first. Leonato's somewhat enigmatical greeting 'trouble being gone, comfort should remain; but when you depart from me, sorrow abides and happiness takes his leave' (I.i.95–97) neatly hints at the tragi-comic mixture of sorrow and happiness, trouble and comfort, which the soldiers' arrival brings to the household and to the play. Don Pedro's question about Hero makes her the focus of attention, on and offstage, with opportunities for the actor playing Innogen (if she is staged) to participate by some gesture when Leonato says 'Her mother hath many times told me so'. The introduction gives Claudio a chance to display his romantic interest in Hero by looks or gestures while Benedick, by contrast, shows off his wit.

110–39 This cues Beatrice's intervention 'I wonder that you will still be talking Signor Benedick; nobody marks you' (I.i.110), a paradox in itself since it shows that she has obviously been watching him closely. The rapid-fire exchange between her and Benedick (I.i.111–39) begins by paying lip service to conventional ceremonial deference in the terms 'Signor Benedick' and the insult 'Lady Disdain'. The couple's mock 'Courtesy' (I.i.110–16) could be displayed effectively by use of flamboyant gestures of greeting: a bow from Benedick (removing his hat) and a responding curtsy from Beatrice. The stichomythia which follows gives each character a chance to proclaim their antipathy to marriage in a parry of insults. If the other characters onstage are all watching Beatrice and Benedick, the stakes in terms of their status are all the higher. If staged as a more private tête à tête, the weird juxtaposition of intimacy and aggression between the two is heightened. Beatrice's bald insult 'scratching could not make it worse, an 'twere such a face as yours were' (I.i.130) marks the degeneration of fine wit into artless (but doubtless heartfelt) malice, marking a loss of status which Benedick quickly capitalises on, dismissing her speech by implying that she is a scold, and calling a close to the conversation with 'I have done' (I.i.137). Her sense of hurt – 'You always end with a jade's trick, I know you of old' (I.i.138–39) – should be given its full weight in performance since it refers back to the previous occasion on which he won her heart with false dice (II.i.257) and tricked her in love.

140–52 At some point in the exchange between Beatrice and Benedick, Don Pedro and Leonato converse apart from the rest of the characters, the latter extending an invitation to the company of soldiers for at least a month. Don Pedro announces this to the assembled company, giving Claudio and Hero the opportunity to exchange coy or more open expressions of delight with the prospect of a continued courtship. Beatrice and Benedick may, by contrast, make extravagant displays of their dismay at seeing more of each other; or, caught off guard, may register their interest in renewed social encounters. Leonato's formal welcome of Don John symbolically marks the entrance of trouble to the house. As a belated greeting, it is uneasy; a pause in performance before Leonato asks Don Pedro 'Please it your grace lead on?' (I.i.152) would point this up. The order in which characters exit into the house will telegraph much about how the dynamics of the greetings have developed over the preceding lines. Leonato and Don Pedro obviously exit together (I.i.153); either Hero and Beatrice follow next or, if Hero expects to welcome Claudio to the house and chooses to linger to send a parting glance or gesture of interest to him, she would follow Don John and his attendants. Claudio must gesture to Benedick to keep him behind onstage, possibly breaking his focus on the parting Beatrice. If Beatrice and Hero exit side by side this would give weight to Benedick's line about Hero 'I noted her not, but I looked on her' (I.i.156).

154–91 Claudio and Benedick remain on the threshold area, Claudio perhaps blocking Benedick's exit after the others or catching his sleeve. Claudio's immature romantic interest is obvious in his need for peer approval of his choice of love object: 'I pray thee tell me truly how thou likest her' (I.i.168–69). His visual and emotional focus should be offstage, to the exit made by Hero, perhaps coercing Benedick to share his point of view in physical terms by taking his arm. Benedick's disbelief at Claudio's affection lures him into an unguarded admission of his attraction to Beatrice who exceeds Hero 'as much in beauty as the first of May doth the last of December' (I.i.181–82). Claudio may be so besotted as not to notice this, but he may raise an eyebrow. Benedick immediately retreats to his defence of bachelorhood. Given that his line 'I hope you have not intent to turn husband – have you?' ends with a question, this could mark a pause before Claudio finally admits (perhaps as much to himself as to Benedick) that he would marry 'if Hero would be my wife' (I.i.185). Benedick's bluster about never seeing a bachelor of threescore again (I.i.188) betrays an anxious insecurity about being alone like Beatrice's later line 'thus goes everyone to the world but I' (II.i.292–93).

192–270 The return of Don Pedro is welcome to Benedick, who fights an increasingly desperate rearguard action defending the all-male community in the following exchange: 'That I neither feel how she should be loved, nor know how she should be worthy is the opinion that fire cannot melt out of me' (I.i.216–18). His determination 'I will live a bachelor' (I.i.230) effectively excludes him from the business of wooing to be negotiated between Claudio and Don Pedro. When Don Pedro asks Benedick to convey a message to Leonato, the confirmed bachelor could retire with signs of relief at having 'almost matter enough in me for such an embassage' (I.i.260).

270–309   The final part of the scene is crucially important in estab-lishing Don Pedro's attitude to the romantic attachments which will dominate the rest of the play. Claudio's suspicion that Don Pedro might be ready to 'fetch me in' or mock him is quickly superseded by a sense that his commanding officer might be able to help and advise him, probably encouraged by Don Pedro's determination to see Benedick 'look pale with love' (I.i.231). Don Pedro's wish to curtail the discussion of Claudio's romantic interests can be played effec-tively as evidence of his own affection for Claudio and fear of losing his love, either from his own sexual interest in the younger man or from a more general love of a younger companion. The physical dis-tance between actors and their movement during this exchange are important ways of communicating the nature of Don Pedro's feelings for his favourite, his sense of disappointment, resignation or self-sacrifice. Any same-sex attraction or non-sexual love of the all-male, locker-room community sits paradoxically with Don Pedro's wish to promote heterosexual matches among others while remaining isolated himself, a confusion which can be subtly telegraphed in performance to give an immediate depth and interest to Don Pedro's character for spectators. His final line 'In practice let us put it presently' (I.i.309) can be delivered with pragmatic enthusiasm, matter-of-fact resigna-tion or a painful sense of loss. It signals an exit, so Don Pedro may pat Claudio on the back or gesture him forward to the house of love. Claudio's excitement about the pursuit of a rich heiress probably means he does not notice Don Pedro's feelings at all.

Act I, scene ii

This short excited exchange in the midst of the bustle of prepara-tions for that evening's dinner and dancing opens with Leonato and Antonio meeting onstage or having done so just offstage. Antonio's news that his servant overheard the last six lines of Don Pedro's speech suggests that a servant should enter at I.i.304 behind the entrance to Leonato's house, perhaps sweeping the entrance or setting up an item such as a torch or candles to show that the party scene takes place at night. The servant's report that 'the prince discovered' that 'he loved my niece your daughter' (I.ii.10–12) and meant to declare it that evening in the dance is the first of many mis-takings and mis-reportings in the play. Antonio's guarded excitement at the prospect of a socially advantageous match is emphasised by his use of the titles 'the prince' and 'Count Claudio', and both brothers refer to the match with a prince as a dream that is not quite to be trusted. Still, Antonio is dispatched to warn Hero while Leonato hurriedly directs his 'cousins', a range of local relations who enter to help prepare the festivities, singling out one 'friend' whose skill he requires. If the production chooses to create a tangible sense of Leonato's domestic world, this could be the director of music whom Leonato was seeking at the opening of the scene, (the actor carrying an instrument), or, alternatively, a cook who is mentioned by Don John in the following scene.

Act I, scene iii

1–37   In contrast to the previous scene, this first private exchange between Don John and his followers is characterised by morose pessimism, stasis and villainous plotting. Setting the exchange in an arbour or under an archway if still outside (where the characters could have been concealed until lit), or in a secluded, perhaps semi-darkened room inside the house, creates the appropriate spatial ambience of confinement and conspiracy that Don John's lines express when he claims 'I am trusted with a muzzle and enfranchised with a clog' (I.iii.30–31). Placing Don John stage right, on the left as seen from in front of the stage, may have associated the character's seclusion with the 'bar sinister' of his illegitimate birth for early modern spectators. Including offstage sounds of revelry makes the point that Don John is not at the feast with the others. Conrade, who declares himself 'born under Saturn' and so morose like his master, could follow Don John's sartorial style by wearing black too, though in less extravagant form. Don John's settled melancholy could be effectively telegraphed by sitting while Conrade, standing, appeals to him. Alternatively, his discontent could be telegraphed through restlessness, moving back and forward across the stage (culling blossoms or leaves from the plants), to show that he cannot 'take true root' (I.iii.22) in Don Pedro's favour and would 'rather be a canker in a hedge than a rose in his grace' (I.iii.25–26). He sets out his stall as the play's villain with no equivocation, and with the opportunity to challenge the audience directly in the lines 'though I cannot be said to be a flattering honest man' (uttered with contempt), 'it must not be denied but I am a plain-dealing villain' as he outlines his determination to bite if he has a chance (I.iii.28–33). His closing, determined self-definition 'let me be that I am, and seek not to alter me' could include the audience as well as Conrade (I.iii.33–34).

38–69 Borachio's entrance breaks the stasis with news from the feast, emphasising Don John's exclusion or self-exclusion since he feels it is partly a celebration of his defeat and so wishes that the 'cook were of my mind' and would poison the guests (I.iii.66–68). The 'intelligence' Borachio brings of an intended wedding is mocked by Don John. His natural antipathy to marriage makes him declare 'What is he for a fool that betroths himself to unquietness' (44–45), ironic since Hero is characterised primarily by her modest silence. Don John's jealousy of Claudio as Don Pedro's 'right hand' (while Don John is 'left' out by his bastardy) may be signalled by his getting up or focusing malevolent attention on Borachio to find out more. Even the quality of overhearing or 'noting' is changed in this sinister scene. Borachio claims he eavesdropped on the prince and Claudio discussing the match in a 'musty room' (I.iii.55), perhaps a hint that Don Pedro needs to secretly remind Claudio of his good intentions. Don John's determination to make his displeasure against the 'young start-up' an excuse to feed his revenge cues his own malevolent entrance to the feast.

Act II

Act II, scene i

Enter* LEONATO, *his brother* [ANTONIO], HERO *his daughter and* BEAT-RICE *his niece.   This scene, in which the characters are bedecked in their finest clothes for the ball, should be spectacular and charged

with an atmosphere of expectation as characters anticipate Don
Pedro and his companions pursuing their romantic interests. It
should appeal to spectators on visual and aural levels, through
the costumes, masks, music and dancing as well as through the
witty dialogue. The mood varies in waves of relaxed banter and
highly charged, tense silences. Leonato's first line 'Was not Don
John here at supper?' (II.i.1) gives continuity with the end of the
previous scene, suggesting the actors cross paths with those exiting. It is spoken with the care of a host, on entering the stage as if
from the dining hall (the characters perhaps carrying glasses, and
Antonio his mask). The setting needs to allow for dancing so may
be in a courtyard, resembling an early modern English banquet-
ing house, a specially designated venue for after-dinner entertain-
ments often located in the gardens of great country houses. This
could be set with minimal changes to the Act I threshold – lights
or torches and chairs for Leonato, Antonio, Beatrice and Hero.
Costume changes, if affordable in production, will effectively suggest evening dress and a party atmosphere full of expectation and
excitement. There may be seating onstage or above for musicians.
These should enter as the scene is set, and then be acknowledged
by Leonato as part of his organisation of the revels. Following the
first entrance, doors or a curtain should close to prepare for the
spectacular entrance of the maskers at line 75.

1–15   The characters establish themselves in the dancing arena;
Leonato may sit at the side of the stage since he is not scripted in
the dancing. Beatrice and Hero could practise a turn or step during the conversation about a man half-way between Benedick and
Don John, since Beatrice refers to 'a good leg and a good foot' in her
flirtatious construction of a man who would 'win any woman in
the world – if 'a could get her good will' (II.i.14–15). The importance
Beatrice places on consent – 'if [he] could get her good will' – could
be effectively marked by a stop and telegraphed kinaesthetically by
Beatrice breaking off her practice dance, or by verbal emphasis or
both. Leonato's protest 'niece, thou wilt never get thee a husband
if thou be so shrewd of thy tongue' (II.i.16–17) may express genuine
concern about her marriage prospects (a perfectly legitimate point
of view for her guardian). Since Leonato knows her so well, it could
also be the prompt for a familiar but ever-witty expression of her

antipathy to marriage, which he knows will be entertaining even if it is a cause for concern.

16–75 Beatrice's uncles, apparently widowers (unless Innogen is also onstage contributing non-verbally to the topic of arranging marriages), are at ease joking about 'horns' or cuckoldry. Beatrice's own desires are paradoxically established through her dislike of a mature man with a beard, whom she would probably not find easy to dominate, and her objections to a young man 'without a beard' whom she could probably control but who, implicitly, might not be adequate to satisfy her sexual appetite. Her determination to go to heaven and sit among the bachelors is not an antipathy to men but to the principle of female subjection in marriage, expressed in her line 'Would it not grieve a woman to be overmastered with a piece of valiant dust?' (II.i.53–54).

Leonato's reminder to Hero that 'If the prince do solicit you in that kind, you know your answer' (II.i.58–60) picks up on Antonio's previous intervention 'Well niece, I trust *you* will be ruled by your father' (II.i.45) (emphasis added). Both are unwelcome comments to Hero if the production has established non-verbally that she reciprocates Claudio's romantic interest. She may enter looking subdued, disappointed or nervous at having to accept Don Pedro's suit, as Leonato has already directed. Beatrice jokes that her cousin might politely promote her own interests by making 'another curtsy and say "Father, as it please me"' (II.i.49, thus hinting at a developing relationship between Hero and Claudio). Hero makes no verbal agreement. Looking down or away could emphasise her reluctance to acknowledge the proposed match. Beatrice, as confidante to Hero's romantic interests, encourages a subversive outmanoeuvring of Don Pedro's suit if he is too importunate: 'tell him there is measure in everything and so dance out the answer' (II.i.62–64). To avoid being contradicted, she launches into another witty set piece, which uses the trope of dancing to describe what she sees as an inevitable decline from the hasty, fantastic wooing ('a Scotch jig' II.i.66) to the stately tradition of the wedding ceremony ('mannerly modest as a measure' II.i.67–68) and finally the days of ever increasing 'Repentance' in married life, compared to the 'cinquepace' (a dance of five paces followed by a leap). It would not be easy for Beatrice to perform steps from these dances while speaking, but her lines prepare for the action to follow, alerting spectators to the symbolic significance of the dance as part of courtship rituals for the couples.

Enter DON PEDRO, CLAUDIO, BENEDICK, BALTHASAR *[masked, with a Drum,* MARGARET *and* URSULA] *and* DON JOHN, [BORACHIO *and others. Music and dancing begin*]   The maskers' entrance up centre stage should be spectacular, heralded by a musical cue, a drum, and by the drawing of curtains or opening of doors to reveal them in tableau, followed by Leonato's announcement 'The revellers are entering, brother' (II.i.74), which cues Antonio to put on his own mask and the maskers to move downstage. Margaret and Ursula also need to enter here if they have not done so earlier (there is no stage direction for them to enter in the quarto text), their different social status perhaps being signalled by actions of refilling wine glasses and passing round the sweetmeats or delicacies typical of an early modern post-dinner 'banquet'. The men's identities are disguised from on and offstage audiences by full masks to increase the frisson of the exchanges between dance partners. A musical intro-duction allows the maskers to make their entrance down the depth of the stage, approach and bow to their prospective partners and lead them into their respective starting positions in the dancing space centre stage. Given his morose nature, Don John may conspicuously position himself apart from the dancers, poised like a crow, stage right, to watch Claudio and intervene at II.i.146.

The next 65 lines of courtship dialogue work most effectively when punctuated by the movements of a dance, a pavan being the most appropriate to mirror the turns in the conversation (Brissenden). The pavan's measured pace easily allows for dialogue between actors, while its pattern of advance and retreat and turns and returns mirrors the step-by-step formality of formal courtship designed to control what Beatrice called the 'fantastic' or excited flow of emotions and desire between the characters. A progressive form of pavan – where a line of women (stage left) are set opposite a line of men (stage right) and at the end of each figure (8 bars of 4 beats) the dancers cast off and move upstage to the back of the line – allows for whoever is speaking to be at the front of the stage.

76–89   Don Pedro identifies himself to an offstage audience when he takes Hero onto the dance floor to stand at the front. His opening line 'Lady, will you walk a bout [a turn] with your friend?' (II.i.76) and her reply should be timed so that her line 'when I walk away' is spoken as the couple take a step apart to the side and his 'With me in your company' comes as they step together again (II.i.79–80). Hero's comment that she will only welcome a partner's company 'when I please' and 'when I like your favour' (II.i.81–84) suggests she is using the protection offered by the mask to follow Beatrice's advice on evading Don Pedro's attentions while still engaging in a deferred flirtation.

89–100   A textual and production choice must be made in assignation of the men's lines in the next exchange with Margaret (II.i.89–100) since the quarto assigns the first three of the male partner's lines to Benedick, transferring to Balthasar for 'Amen' and the final 'No more words; the clerk is answered' (II.i.97–100). Assuming that the change is due to compositorial error in the printing shop gives the director (like the editor) the opportunity to give all the lines to one male partner. Pairing Margaret with Balthasar throughout preserves the ordered progress of the dance, so emphasising its kinaesthetic power to hold couples together in playful tension. If all the lines are given to one actor, a more logical pairing for Margaret is with Borachio, who is in her favour (II.ii.12). If, however, the director chooses to follow the pattern of mixed speech prefixes from Q, the initial flirting between Benedick and Margaret sets a precedent for their later exchanges. When Balthasar (or Borachio) cuts in on the dance, the exchange physically enacts jealous intervention and thus forms a parallel with Claudio's more passive jealousy of Don Pedro's dancing with Hero.

101–12   Antonio and probably Ursula, too, are dancers of an older generation. Ursula's familiarity with Antonio suggests her status in Leonato's household: probably an old retainer or housekeeper who stands in place of the missing mother. Ursula insults and flatters Antonio with a mature confidence rather than the frisson of uncertainty between the younger couples. This teasing draws on long-time acquaintance – 'I know thee well enough' (II.i.101) – and makes the important dramatic point that the masks are thin disguises. It leads straight into …

113–40   Beatrice and Benedick's movement to the head of the dance and front of the stage. Via an artful exchange of wit both characters play on the complex fiction of not knowing who their partner is while simultaneously recognising each other and knowing that they have been recognised. Since their conversation is twice as long as those which have preceded it, they will either need 16 bars of music to dance while speaking, or they could be left stationary at the front of the stage after the dance completes, or while the others dance it through again. In the latter case, Beatrice's remark 'We must follow the leaders' (II.i.137) recognises that they have dropped out of the dance because of her description of Benedick as 'the Prince's jester' (II.i.125), and that she is now ready to rejoin it. If Benedick asks her 'I pray you, what is he?' in anticipation or hope of hearing something good about himself from Beatrice, his hope is vain in all senses of the word, and some non-verbal expression of disappointment at her insults would be appropriate. Beatrice exploits the freedom which a mask gives to the wearer, confiding to Benedick 'None but libertines delight in him, and the commendation is not in his wit but in his villainy' (II.i.126–28), lines that tellingly reveal her bitterness about his former betrayal of her ('with false dice'). It is she who emerges victorious in this verbal skirmish of wit, even though he is taking the lead in the dance. Her resolve to 'leave' at the next turning to avoid 'any ill' (II.i.139–40) perhaps covertly warns him she will not be taken in again. Directors and actors must decide whether Beatrice and Benedick follow the others to rejoin and end the dance (possibly with a reverence), or break from it. The same-sex lines formed in the dance are preserved in the exit. Don Pedro, now at the back of the stage, exits with Leonato, probably followed by Balthasar (if he is Margaret's partner) and Antonio and Benedick, while the women follow Hero. If Borachio dances with Margaret, he returns to Don John.

141–67   Don John's commentary on the exit (II.i.141–3) is a deliberate misinterpretation delivered for Claudio's benefit, as the plotters move towards him. The three of them form a close, predatory group around him (especially effective if they are costumed in non-festive black), purportedly confiding their concern for Don Pedro's honour, but effectively creating a claustrophobic web of lies. Having sown the poison, Don John sociably leads the group off to the banquet, leaving Claudio in his own former position: physically isolated and emotionally excluded from the festivities. Claudio removes his mask to reveal his face in the first two lines of soliloquy. His subsequent words go on to reveal his shallow or immature personality. The lines are a mixture of insecurity, shame and anger which can be spoken as if pondering over what he has just seen and heard to himself, or by actively recruiting members of the audience – who have witnessed the same 'hourly proof' – to share his views that 'Friendship is constant in all other things / Save in the office and affairs of love' and that 'Beauty is a witch / Against whose charms faith melteth into blood' (II.i.160–61 and 164–65). Silence from the audience implicitly confirms his worst suspicions. A performance emphasising a sympathetic interpretation of the young lover could exploit a brief opportunity to show the depth of his sense of loss – and affection for Hero – in the phrase 'Farewell, therefore, Hero'.

168–92 Benedick may, in theory, be quite cavalier about Claudio's sense that his romantic desires have been frustrated. To have Benedick, as confirmed bachelor, patronising the disappointed lover is one way of playing the dialogue between them. More likely, however, Benedick's preoccupation with Beatrice's words to him in the dance means that he does not fully appreciate the seriousness of Claudio's sense of betrayal. He reads Claudio's appearance of sadness as the typical pose of a forlorn or forsaken lover, teasing him about wearing the willow garland, until he is pulled up by Claudio's line 'I wish him [Don Pedro] joy of her'. Benedick's reassurance 'did you think the prince would have used you thus?', accompanied by a gesture such as putting an arm round Claudio's shoulder, prepares for a retaliatory move from Claudio (angrily throwing Benedick's arm off) which Benedick refers to as 'you'll beat the post' (II.i.183 with a pun on post for messenger). Even this and Claudio's petulant exit seem not to capture Benedick's full attention. He returns to ponder on Beatrice's words, contrasting his own merriment with Claudio's lover's sadness. His concern for his reputation ironically reveals that he too puts 'the world into her person' since he is so concerned with Beatrice's opinion (II.i.189–92). Since the lines are about public reputation, actively sharing these ruminations with the audience would be appropriate.

193–252 Benedick's pondering marks a delay, causing Don Pedro's somewhat impatient entrance, probably embarrassed that he, followed by Leonato and the prospective bride, have to seek out Claudio themselves. Benedick's roundabout way of explaining Claudio's absence via the metaphor of the schoolboy and the stolen nest should be addressed covertly and hurriedly to Don Pedro in a further attempt to cover the embarrassment, as the expectant Leonato and Hero look in vain for Claudio. The teasing riddle also allows Benedick to verify Don Pedro's intentions and discredit Claudio's suspicions in a discreet way. To cover the still-conspicuous absence of Claudio, Don Pedro fills time by returning to the safe subject of Beatrice and Benedick's quarrel. Some of Benedick's vituperative remarks, including his vow 'I would not marry her though she were endowed with all that Adam had left him before he transgressed' (II.i.229–31) may be witnessed by Beatrice if she makes an early entrance with Claudio and is stopped in her tracks by what she overhears. Don Pedro alerts Benedick to her entrance, prompting his hyperbolic requests to be sent on a mission to the world's end. These lines are cutting. He constructs himself as a questing knight – possibly with a series of elaborate bows to his Prince, in a perversely unchivalric wish to avoid 'Lady Tongue' (II.i.251). He exits triumphant with this final insult, which is doubtless regarded by Beatrice as another 'jade's trick' (I.i.138) even though his hurry to get offstage shows her the effectiveness of her earlier words.

253–62 Who has won the battle of wits is put into question by Beatrice's surprisingly candid admission about having given her heart to Benedick once before and been wronged (II.i.255–58). A change of tone for these lines allows the actor to give characters and audience a glimpse of Beatrice's sensitivity. A more defensive Beatrice might invent some business – with her fan, mask or hair – to cover the character's embarrassment. Direct address to Don Pedro, exposing her sadness, constitutes an appeal for help. A sensitive Don Pedro may take this as the cue for his determination to undertake one of Hercules' labours at the end of the scene (II.i.336–37).

263–79 The presentation of Claudio and the ensuing betrothal increases rather than diminishes the acute sense of embarrassment onstage. Speech and movement are stilted, often having to be prompted by Beatrice as onstage director. Don Pedro is partly responsible for this, leaving Claudio standing in the belief he has been betrayed (II.i.262–73). A possessive or homosexual Don Pedro, uneasy with betrothals and weddings anyway, can play the lines as though prolonging the last moments of his power over Claudio and deferring the surrender of his favourite. Don Pedro's questions are unnecessary and, played high-status, like those of a master shaming a schoolboy, they expose Claudio's lack of trust. Spoken more gently, they make an appeal to re-establish direct, honest communication. Claudio's refusal to open up should be reflected in his rigid lack of movement, perhaps accompanied by a refusal to look Don Pedro in the eye. This raises the tension until Beatrice breaks the stand-off by stating what Don Pedro already knows. This is hardly a promising start for the betrothal. Hero and Leonato may express their uneasiness facially, and with hesitant movements forward as Don Pedro announces 'Name the day of marriage, and may God give thee joy' (II.i.276).

280–86   Claudio's continued silence after Leonato has formally handed Hero over to him is again deeply embarrassing, even if it is motivated by 'joy' as he claims (II.i.281). The emotional distance between the couple is effectively illustrated by a physical space between them, which may not even be crossed when Claudio formally presents himself to Hero. His lines 'Lady, as you are mine, I am yours. I give away myself for you and dote upon the exchange' (II.i.282–84) sound more like a tennis match, with affections sent back and forth across the court from a distance, than an intimate declaration of love. They produce no response from Hero. She, like Claudio, has to be prompted by Beatrice to move forward and 'stop his mouth with a kiss' (II.i.285–86).

287–305   Any physical contact here to mark the betrothal establishes them as a couple, leaving Leonato looking on indulgently as a proud father and the observers Don Pedro and Beatrice as outsiders. Both register the loss of their closest companions while watching and focusing audience attention on the couple's happiness, centre stage. Both Don Pedro and the normally poised Beatrice are confused by the romantic spectacle. Beatrice's candid wish for a husband is a revelation that probably startles her as much as anyone. Taken aback by Don Pedro's 'Lady Beatrice, I will get you one' she rushes in – as she says 'all mirth and no matter' – to suggest him as her preferred choice and then equally quickly rejects him (II.i.295–303). Played more slowly, each character's longing to enter the married community and deep fear of being excluded in splendid, lonely isolation, becomes apparent. Even though Beatrice knows she is not addressing the man she loves, she may pause to consider Don Pedro's offer in the belief that she can never win Benedick's love. Don Pedro may be wooing for himself, a seriousness signalled if he takes the trouble to kneel and offer his hand, which would produce more embarrassment when Beatrice refuses.

306–20 Beatrice punctures attempts to laugh this off in another desperate bid to transcend her reputation as 'all mirth and no matter' when she firmly tells Don Pedro she was not born in a merry hour: 'No sure, my lord, my mother cried' (II.i.308). Beatrice, orphaned and lonely, could be on the verge of tears as she bids Hero and Claudio 'God give you joy', a possibility strengthened by Leonato's oddly vague line 'Niece, will you look to those things I told you of?' (II.i.311), which provides her with an exit. If so, the men's subsequent refusal to recognise the 'melancholy element' (II.i.316) in Beatrice is doubly ironic, an embarrassment about tears that is not addressed until Act V Scene i. Alternatively, Leonato's dismissal is more abrupt, indicating disapproval and impatience at her rude rejection of the most eligible bachelor she could wish for. She pointedly asks for Leonato's mercy and for Don Pedro's pardon when leaving the stage, probably with a formal curtsy in an attempt to re-establish the illusion of decorum.

321–58 Don Pedro, if played as a matchmaker rather than a lonely melancholic, may already have his plot in mind when he promises Beatrice 'I will get you one [a Husband]'. If so, his proposal is flippant with no accompanying gesture, a throw-away remark designed to test out her affection for Benedick. Heartened by her response, Don Pedro concentrates his energies on fashioning a match to coincide with Hero and Claudio's wedding and to provide a distraction in the intervening days. Hero and Claudio's non-verbal interactions following their betrothal give actors a chance to demonstrate the attraction that later produces such an extreme sense of betrayal for each of the characters. Claudio's impulsive eagerness to marry 'tomorrow' (II.i.229) nevertheless betrays the same schoolboy immaturity that ensures the effectiveness of Don John's plots. Leonato, the host (whose earlier request to Beatrice could be explained with reference to arrangements for the impending wedding), should register a degree of shock at this proposal and intervene quickly to set a more sensible timescale, showing relief when Don Pedro approves this. Finally, the scene reaches a moment where the atmosphere is, albeit briefly, one of harmony and happy expectation. Don Pedro builds on this, taking centre stage and drawing the others physically closer to him as he reveals his plan to deceive Beatrice and Benedick. The grouping of actors in creative plotting should mirror the earlier predatory group around Claudio and the scene to follow with Don John.

Act II, scene ii

A direct contrast is set up to the happy, expansive ending to Act II scene i, orchestrated by Don Pedro, and this scene in which Don John's malice is the forge for destructive desires. A change of lighting as Don Pedro and his group exit, and Don John enters with Borachio and possibly Conrade too, can telegraph the dramatic change of mood. The festive costumes worn by Don Pedro's group for the masked ball contrast with the darker tones worn by the malcontented bastard brother and his companions.

1–52   Don John's opening line 'It is so, the Count Claudio shall marry the daughter of Leonato' may be literally a passing comment on the couple as they leave the stage and he enters. The betrothal marks the failure of his initial plot, of course. Pacing about the stage (II.ii.4–7), his frustration and anger at failing to take revenge on Claudio is clear. Don John identifies himself with the typical malcontent who is 'sick in displeasure' (II.ii.5) to his adversary. Claudio had, of course, been instrumental in putting down Don John's rebellion. In addition, Don John's bitterness about marriage and his wish for 'any cross, any impediment' to destroy it is explained by his illegitimacy. While Don Pedro explains his creative design to others, Don John is more like a black hole, sucking a deceptive plot from Borachio that will feed his displeasure. He obviously holds social power over Borachio, yet is dependent on him for creative ideas, a paradox in status that is reflected in the perverse yoking of binary opposites in the language. Borachio flatters his superior by telling Don John that the 'life' of the plot to cause the 'death of this marriage' lies in his ability to 'poison' the scene that Borachio will present before Don Pedro and Claudio. It is Borachio who directs Don John, giving him detailed instructions on what to say, how to deliver the speeches, and what pretended motivation to adopt (II.ii.30–46). By accompanying his directions with non-verbal signs of deference, such as a brief bow, Borachio preserves the illusion of status difference. Don John's perverse eagerness to hear how the plot will engender 'adverse issue' climaxes with his determination to 'put it in practice' (II.ii.47–48). He leaves the stage 'to learn their day of marriage' (II.ii.52) with confident strides and a much clearer sense of direction than he had at the beginning of the scene where his anger eddied in circles of frustration. Despite its common attribution to Don John, the plot is really Borachio's, who may smile at the audience before making his own, more leisurely exit.

Act II, scene iii

Offering many opportunities for comic effects, this overhearing scene takes place outside Leonato's house in an orchard that includes an arbour or recess where Benedick can hide. From the simplest effects of background birdsong and a gobo of green leaf patterns projected onto the stage, to movable pieces suggesting trees or hedges, some change of scene must be indicated. Its lightness should contrast with the menacing dark atmosphere of the previous scene. A network of criss-crossed branch and leaf shadows on the stage floor would effectively suggest the trap or snare in which Don Pedro is hoping to trap Benedick, as indicated by Claudio's imagery of hunting (II.iii.94 and 110). In a Western tradition going back to the Song of Songs in the Bible, the garden is a classic *locus amoenus*, a place of sensual love, and given Don Pedro's confident assertion that Cupid's glory 'shall be ours, for we are the only love-gods' (II.i.237), a statue of Cupid the archer would be an appropriate piece of moveable scenery.

1–7 Benedick's dispatch of his boy to bring him a book from his room to the orchard immediately establishes that this is a place of leisure. Indeed, the orchard's associations with the leisure enjoyed in Paradise can be invoked to suggest that Don Pedro has orchestrated a secular 'fortunate fall' into love for Benedick.

8–34 Benedick's soliloquy verbalises the shift from the work of war to the leisured play of love on which *Much Ado* is founded. It is a change personified by Claudio, 'Monsieur Love' (II.iii.34), that Benedick does not like: 'there was no music with him but the drum and the fife, and now he had rather hear the tabor and the pipe' (II.iii.13–14). The soliloquy's length is itself indicative of the time

Benedick now has on his hands – a note of boredom or frustration in his tone carries echoes of Don John's antipathy to love. He might wander round the orchard, possibly picking up an apple as he chats. Previous scenes have amply demonstrated that Benedick is pleased by the sound of his own voice, so there is nothing odd in his talking over to himself the new environment in which he must operate. Choosing to address and engage the audience, however, creates a much more interesting dynamic in the scene. First, it gives the actor a chance to 'recruit' spectators as substitute military companions to replace those he has now lost. He gossips with the audience about Claudio's behaviour, clothes, speech as a lover. Delivering these lines in the proximity of, or with reference to a statue of Cupid, allows for dismissive gestures to emphasise his disdain. His second 'locker-room' subject, confidently detailing his immunity to love for any woman, no matter how many of the womanly graces she holds, should be even more of a bravura performance – involving movement and the singling out of individual spectators to witness his statements. Its effect is highly ironic since his fall from proud singularity is imminent. Taking a bite of one of the orchard apples after he asks 'May I be so converted and see with these eyes?' (II.iii.21) would point this up. The audience already know the answer. Their superior knowledge adds a second comic effect to an actor's choice of direct address in the soliloquy. Benedick mistakenly thinks he has co-opted them as exclusive confidants to his perspective on events, whereas spectators enjoy a superior omniscience by sharing also the viewpoint of the plotters Don Pedro, Leonato and Claudio.

35–41 Their entrance surprises Benedick and his chosen hiding place in the 'arbour' should not be very effective for it is important that the audience see his non-verbal reactions. As well as fostering Benedick's illusion of camaraderie with spectators, a downstage position maximises the opportunity for the actor to use facial expressions as well as small gestures to convey his surprise and excitement at what he overhears. Don Pedro, Leonato and Claudio enter with the purpose of locating Benedick, but in a leisurely manner to give an appearance of relaxation. This is fostered by Don Pedro's request for Balthasar, the singer and musician, to play. The stage direction for 'Jack Wilson' instead of Balthasar's entrance in the Folio text establishes that *'with music'* indicates a musical instrument rather than an accompanying band of musicians. Claudio's comment 'How still the evening is' (II.iii.36), gesturing around to the still trees (and casting an eye to spot Benedick), refers to his own romantic mood and, more strategically, to the fact that these are ideal conditions to overhear the music and their words. The subsequent two lines, delivered in conspiratorial, excited stage whispers, celebrate a boys' practical joke, with the reference to Benedick as 'a kid-fox worth a pennyworth' (II.iii.40) perhaps referring to the childhood game 'Fox-in-a-hole' (McEachern, 2007, 208). Perhaps Benedick is standing dangerously balanced on one leg, leaning forward to hear at this point, as children did in this hopping game.

41–90 The witty banter in which Don Pedro woos Balthasar to sing needs to be lively with an immediate pick-up of cue lines, and yet spoken pointedly enough to give shape to the unusual dynamic played out between singer and patron, and to draw attention to hints about the play's themes. The Prince of Aragon here adopts the position of wooer to his servant, perhaps tempting Balthasar with the illusion or hope of a more intimate relationship with his master, though the musician shows scepticism about the wooing process in his lines 'Since many a wooer doth commence his suit / To her he thinks not worthy, yet he woos, / Yet will he swear he loves' (II.iii.48–50). It is Claudio who commences his suit to a woman he later rejects as unworthy, of course, so this and Balthasar's lyric 'Men were deceivers ever … To one thing constant never' (II.iii.61–63) advertises the dangers to come. It also betrays the dangerous desire to preserve exclusively homosocial bonds which underlies the potential tragedy. Benedick seems to have an inkling of this, and his aside 'I pray God his bad voice bode no mischief' should underline the point for the audience. Since, as Stuart Gillespie and Bruce Smith have remarked (2006), the performance of song merges its emotional content with the body, voice and passions of the performer, Balthasar's singing may be a personal plea against heterosexual wooing. If Balthasar does entertain the possibility of a more intimate relationship with Don Pedro, then the latter's pointed dismissal of him – 'Farewell', spoken because Balthasar does not immediately leave the stage to follow Don Pedro's order to 'get us some excellent music' with which to woo Hero – is brusque. Balthasar is not admitted to the boys' conspiracy against Benedick. Balthasar's purportedly dismissive comment 'there's not a note of mine that's worth the noting' (with a pun created by the Elizabethan pronunciation of 'nothing' with a long *o*), self-consciously draws attention to the way in which art can strategically shape people and events. Checking the tuning of his instrument (which must be stringed for him to sing and play) gives material grounds for his repetition of the word 'note'. His pun tunes into the immediate 'overhearing' context as well as the play's title. Benedick's scorn that others are moved by music 'that sheep guts should hale souls out of men's bodies', can be supplemented by non-verbal signs of exasperation during the song itself. This sets him up as a target for Cupid's arrow.

91–155 Don Pedro's 'Come hither Leonato' (II.iii.91) cues a move closer to Benedick's hiding place as well as the beginning of the prearranged dialogue, the first stage of which introduces the idea of Beatrice's love-sickness for Benedick (II.iii.91–155). The ruse is so effective because the plotters first preempt Benedick's own scepticism by invoking the idea that Beatrice's love is only counterfeit, and then use Leonato to dismiss this possibility.

As an older character, Leonato's inventive facility may not be as quick as Claudio and Don Pedro's, and the ensuing dialogue offers opportunity for non-verbal comic business as Don Pedro and Claudio prompt him to speak, knowing that his testimony is crucial in suggesting veracity. As Benedick makes clear, 'I should think this a gull, but that the white-bearded fellow speaks it' (II.i.119–21). Leonato appears to be stuck for an answer to Don Pedro's leading question 'What effects of passion shows she?' but Don Pedro and Claudio are quick to exploit the improvisatory possibilities offered by his stalling comment 'you heard my daughter tell you how' (II.iii.109–12). Claudio's 'She did indeed', followed by Don Pedro's 'You amaze me' implies that something rather risqué has been whispered, and the whispering draws Benedick out of his hiding place in order to try to overhear this too. Claudio's line 'bait the hook well, this fish will bite' (II.iii.110) could also imply that the whispering has been set up in advance (to lure Benedick nearer), rather than making a virtue out of necessity when Leonato 'dries' or forgets his lines. Claudio's aside 'He hath ta'en the infection; hold it up' suggests Benedick has now made a physical move into the open. He is more vulnerable to love, to the bait, and more vulnerable to exposure in physical terms too. The actor's attempt to hide behind the statue of Cupid (or behind a tree) while the plotters move around it in discussion creates the opportunity for farce as he tries to get closer to the conversation and avoid being seen. Quick movements round the statue, or pulling a branch in a vain attempt to hide himself can create laughter. The more ineffective these are, the greater the comic effect. By means of conspiratorial smiles, nudges and winks, the others can show their enjoyment of Benedick's eagerness to find out as much as he can – even swallowing an old joke about himself and Beatrice 'between the sheets' of a letter (II.iii.136–39).

155–211 The second part of the overhearing script involves the praise of Beatrice, producing quieter, more reflective responses from Benedick. Even though the dialogue is deliberately staged, there is nothing to suggest that the plotters' admiration is not genuine. These are complements which they would not dare to offer in public for fear of a sharp reproof. Don Pedro's words 'I would she had bestowed this dotage on me. I would have doffed all other respects and made her half myself' carries extra resonance in the light of his earlier proposal. If it was serious, the line carries a poignant sense of his rejection. Claudio's playfully salacious references to the fact that Beatrice 'will die' (II.iii.170) raise the erotic temperature for Benedick, whose handkerchief may be produced to wipe his brow (and then cover his face if the plotters move suddenly nearer to him). He should react vehemently to the view that he 'hath a contemptible spirit' – perhaps spluttering to make the handkerchief move – and coming dangerously close to exposing his presence (II.iii.177). He then retreats to listen more thoughtfully to his friends' opinions that he is wise and valiant but 'should modestly examine himself' (II.iii.201), which carefully cues his soliloquy. The plotters' resignation to Beatrice's hopeless position (II.iii.195–200), accompanied by sad shakes of the head, or patting Leonato on the shoulder as they exit, leaves Benedick poised (as he thinks) in the high-status position of being able to graciously change his attitude to love.

205–35 Benedick comes forward from his hiding place and/or removes his handkerchief to appeal to the audience again as witnesses to corroborate what he has just heard. Excitement and delight are barely tempered by the illusory logic of reasoning that structures his sentences. He adopts a morally self-righteous tone in the lines 'I must not seem proud. Happy are they that hear their detractions and can put them to mending' (II.iii.220–22). The eagerness of Benedick's resolution 'I will be horribly in love with her' (II.iii.226–27) is pointed up by a determined exit at this point, before he realises the probable consequences of his change of attitude and turns back to consider 'I may chance have some odd quirks and remnants of wit broken on me ... ' (II.iii.227–28). The last few lines reason with the audience and build towards a triumphant determination – to be married – as though this were the only logical conclusion. Benedick's self-assurance should be telegraphed through tone and stance – an open, upright stance, arms akimbo perhaps, or with a conclusive action like taking another bite of his apple – to cover Beatrice's entrance.

236 *Enter* BEATRICE Beatrice is irritated at having been sent to summon Benedick (who had previously left the stage begging to be dismissed from her presence) to dinner. Signs of annoyance in her gait, facial expression and gestures – such as sweeping her train or vigorously waving her fan – make Benedick's spying of 'some marks of love in her' (II.iii.237) all the more ridiculous. She registers momentary shock at his smile and thanks, before assuming this is meant sarcastically. She squares herself opposite him for another battle of wit and, either angered or bemused by his suggestion that she takes 'pleasure' in the message, delivers a loaded shot in her jibe about the jackdaw which pointedly critiques his sadistic cruelty. It is followed by what is, to her, a mysterious pause, as he does not retaliate – though he may continue to smile. Her parting question 'You have no stomach, signor? Fare you well' (II.ii.246–47) could refer to the apple in his hand as well as his lack of appetite for a parry of wit, and she closes the encounter with a brisk exit, perhaps snapping her fan shut or flicking her train behind her first. Benedick watches her exit intently, completely unconscious that his reading of the situation is wildly out of kilter with what the audience have just seen. He rushes offstage after her to 'get her picture' (II.iii.254), fully transformed into an obsessed lover.

Act III

Act III, scene i

This woman-centred parallel to the previous overhearing scene takes place in the orchard too.

1–23   Hero asks Margaret to direct Beatrice to hide in 'the pleached bower' where the thick honeysuckle prevents the sun from entering 'like favourites / Made proud by princes that advance their pride / Against the sun that bred it' (III.i.7–11). These words are often cut, but can carry immediate dramatic resonance if spoken in the same spot that Balthasar and Don Pedro had their exchange (II.iii.41–55). To point up the dramatic and gender oppositions, and to avoid an exact repetition of actions, Beatrice's hiding place should be at the opposite side of the stage to Benedick's, a parallel arbour down stage right. Don Pedro may have arranged the plot but Hero's vocabulary firmly identifies their women's 'discourse' which is 'all of her' [Beatrice] (III.i.5–6) in opposition to the men's conversation in the 'parlour' (III.i.1). Hero outlines a strategy to Ursula while walking away from the arbour (so Beatrice can enter secretly), and if the production has a statue of Cupid she can walk towards this for the reference to 'little Cupid's crafty arrow' (III.i.22), as the two wait.

Enter BEATRICE   A slight pause, as Ursula and Hero look offstage in search of Beatrice, heightens the comedy of Beatrice's hasty entrance, running close to the ground 'like a lapwing' and dodging between trees, potted bushes, or plants in an attempt to stay concealed.

23–33   If Hero's outline of the plot has been seriously earnest, Beatrice's entrance can produce smothered smiles and giggles. Hero has just over two lines to speak in a stage whisper to Ursula and Ursula replies with a further six, allowing plenty of time for comic business (III.i.23–31). Once Beatrice is settled and attentive, they move downstage close to the hiding place 'that her ear lose nothing' (III.i.32).

34–48   The women's staged conversation follows the same strategy as in the previous scene of preempting scepticism, criticising the eavesdropper and praising the beloved. If, as the script implies, Ursula is an older character who has substituted for Hero's mother in the role of housekeeper, then she functions, like Leonato, as a figure whose words lend veracity to what is spoken. Ursula's name invokes the mother bear who licks her infants (the younger women Hero and Beatrice) into shape. Her protestation 'are you sure / That Benedick loves Beatrice so entirely' could produce a spontaneous reaction of surprise from Beatrice, who may involuntarily stick her head out of the arbour like a lapwing sticking its head up from the nest. A small cry, followed by a hand clapped over her mouth and immediate withdrawal to the arbour, would give Ursula and Hero the chance for some fun in momentarily glancing up at the trees in search of the bird who made the strange call. Beatrice should also react to the advice that she should never be told about Benedick's infatuation (III.i.40–44). If she partly emerges from the hiding place again with a tendril of honeysuckle round her hat as a token disguise, she is fully exposed to react to the erotic charge (and rhythm) of Ursula's line that Benedick deserves 'as full and fortunate a bed / As ever Beatrice shall couch upon' (III.i.45–46). Hero's next line prolongs the fantasy moment – 'O god of love! I know he doth deserve / As much as may be yielded to a man' (III.i.47–48) – and Beatrice could sigh, roll her eyes upwards to show how she is secretly excited by the prospect.

49–86   Hero's subsequent critique of Beatrice's assertive independence as pride, scorn and disdain comes as a serious shock. Beatrice expects her uncle and the other men to find her proto-feminist stance unacceptable, but to hear Ursula and Hero agree in judging it 'not commendable' seriously undermines what she has always stood for (III.i.71). It is not just her wit to 'turn every man the wrong side out' or her sharp tongue that are criticised. Hero speaks as if straight from a conduct book in suggesting that 'to be so odd and from all fashions / As Beatrice is cannot be commendable' (III.i.72–73). Beatrice realises that her adamant determination not to be subjected in marriage or 'overmastered with a piece of valiant dust' since 'Adam's sons are my brethren' is not recognised by her 'sisters' for the radical, feminist claims to equality it makes (II.i.54–57). To indicate shock, disappointment and even shame, Beatrice could physically close up in response to this attack. She may move defensively backwards or into the arbour. Hero probably does not realise the extent of the sting in her words though, as she implies, the overhearing scene does give her a freedom to express things she would not dare to say directly to Beatrice. Her idea of finding honest slanders to 'stain my cousin withal' (III.i.84–85) is a deeply ironic reflection of the collapse of proto-feminist power that this scene stages.

87–99   The more mature Ursula, having noted Beatrice's reaction, quickly steps in with 'O, do not do your cousin such a wrong' (III.i.87) and turns the conversation round in praise of Beatrice's wit, which should lead to good judgement. A move closer to the actor playing Beatrice to ensure this more positive judgement is heard can make the actor open up a little to show that Beatrice's attention is re-engaged. Since she obviously values Hero and Ursula's opinions, she might register her pleasure in hearing their commendations of Signor Benedick as 'so rare a gentleman' (III.i.87–91). Ursula's 'fancy' that Benedick 'goes foremost in report though Italy' is one certainly shared by Beatrice who could nod – either vigorously or more thoughtfully – as a physical testament of her belief in his 'excellence' (III.i.97–99). If so, Ursula and Hero can take time to notice this, with smiles to each other, before breaking off from their set piece.

100–106 Their parting lines are no more innocent than the rest. Ursula's pointed reference to Hero's imminent wedding plays cleverly on Beatrice's earlier cry '"hey ho for a husband"' (II.i.294) and her wish to be in fashion with the life patterns of her cousin and other women, rather than out of it. To point up her exclusion, Hero and Ursula could exit arm in arm, pointedly ignoring the 'problem' of Beatrice as they move on, supposedly in excited discussion of the more important matter of which gown and accessories should be chosen for the wedding. Hero's aside 'Some Cupid kills with arrows, some with traps' (III.i.106), which could be delivered as they pass the statue, offers the chance for a last backward glance to enjoy the success of their plotting.

107–16 Beatrice's soliloquy is much less triumphant, much more reflective than Benedick's prose soliloquy in the previous scene, and the verse gives her lines a measured quality. This can be shown in action if Beatrice emerges slowly and questioningly from her hiding place. Her first concern is with her reputation; she struggles to accept the implications of Hero and Ursula's words. 'Stand I condemned for pride and scorn so much?' could be spoken with a glance after them and should reflect the pain their criticisms have inflicted. It is their lack of faith in her which makes her bid 'maiden pride, adieu', recognising with deep regret – and a sigh – that 'No glory lives behind the back of such' (III.i.109–10). Bubbling under her sense of sisterly betrayal is Beatrice's joy that she is loved by Benedick, as reflected in the verse. Its two quatrains and couplet are a compressed sonnet. The actor could physically turn to indicate Beatrice's ideological turn to meet the future when delivering the 'turn' line that opens the second quatrain: 'And Benedick, love on, I will requite thee / Taming my wild heart to thy loving hand' (III.i.111–12). The tone of this line could be determined rather than excited, though the double stress on 'wild heart' suggests the passion of Beatrice's pounding heart, barely governed by her reason. Her feelings of desire emerge in the following two lines of the quatrain that culminates with thoughts of the 'holy band' of marriage – ideally spoken in a single breath to reflect that growing excitement. The character (and actor) then need to take a deep breath to assimilate – and enjoy – the full import of this newly imagined future life-path. Beatrice's final couplet is one of assurance on many levels: already assured that others find Benedick deserving, she rises above the eavesdropping plot in the enjambement hinged with a micro-pause at the line break in 'I / Believe it better than reportingly' where she fully acknowledges her feelings (III.i.115–16). She reassures the audience that she believes in Benedick from her own judgement and feelings, so the overhearing plot is not an imposition but a means of recognition. This return to her independent judgement gives her the self-assurance to release her passion for Benedick anew, overcoming her fears of those 'false dice' (II.i.257) from the past. Beatrice exits confidently, with barely controlled excitement that puts a spring into her step.

Act III, scene ii

This scene is pivotal in several ways: it marks the shift from all-male camaraderie and single life to marriage, which inevitably leaves Don Pedro isolated, and the turn from comedy to potential tragedy which Don John's news brings. It is set in or around Leonato's house and can be done with a minimum or no change of scenery if it is to follow straight on from the previous scene. If the orchard setting has a statue, retaining it gives extra irony to Don Pedro's reference to Cupid (III.ii.9–11) and Benedick's supposed immunity to love.

1–7   Don Pedro enters perhaps with an affectionate arm around his favourite, Claudio, and promises to 'stay until your marriage be consummate' before going home to Aragon alone (III.ii.1–2). Early modern marriage rituals went beyond the church ceremony right up to the bedding of the newly married couple, so there would be nothing extraordinary in these words for original audiences. The sexual sense of 'consummated' can signal this as a moment of painfully anticipated loss on Don Pedro's part, however. Claudio naively tries to maintain the illusion of camaraderie by offering to accompany Don Pedro back home (perhaps sensing what a break this will be for them both), but his offer is brushed off as Don Pedro adopts a paternal tone (III.ii.5–7). The actor could pat Claudio on the shoulder before removing his arm, turning away from Claudio and back to the actors who follow, as Don Pedro seeks out Benedick.

8–29   If Don Pedro is disguising his real feelings, the actor can telegraph suppressed emotion under the bluff joke that Benedick 'hath a heart as sound as a bell, and his tongue is the clapper: for what his heart thinks, his tongue speaks' (III.ii.11–13). Don Pedro's lines summon Benedick forward, offering an opportunity to reveal the character's complete transformation from soldier to lover as he moves centre stage. In order to protect himself from comment, Benedick may try to minimise his presence, the actor curling his body in on itself and holding his hand over his face to disguise the removal of Benedick's beard by the barber. The line 'Gallants, I am not as I have been' may be muffled. The three plotters circle him with amusement, curious about why he is covering his face and sceptical about his 'toothache' (III.ii.20–27). Benedick withdraws further in reaction to Claudio's suggestion 'he is in love', rightly anticipating how he will be teased, but Don Pedro's cleverly strategic remark 'There is no appearance of fancy in him' may then lure him into opening up again.

30–39   If the actor stands up straight here, he can reveal his fashionable clothes or 'strange disguises' to Don Pedro's amused scrutiny. The costume must display a version of the named items: a pair of extra large and flamboyant gathered trousers; a clearly displayed and possibly highly embroidered shirt (the notable lack of doublet reflecting sartorially the exposure of his vulnerable breast and heart beneath the shirt). The lover's emotional exposure can be made more tantalising by the addition of a rich Spanish cape hanging off the shoulder to allow a glimpse of the soft shirt, and to draw attention to the passionate heart beneath. The early modern German or Dutch fashion for very large, fully gathered 'slops' or breeches makes it impossible for Benedick to make himself inconspicuous of course (see pp. 99–100). To fashion-conscious spectators at the end of the 16th century, the mixture of Dutch slops and a Spanish cloak would have been utterly incongruous, as Don Pedro's lines point out. The same grotesque effect can be achieved in productions designed in different historical periods or with contemporary dress, by a choice of garments that display a very obvious and inappropriate clash of styles. Clashing colours can emphasise the inelegant figure cut by Benedick, whose unease in the costume of a lover should also be clear from his difficulty in moving around the stage, or even standing up in these unfamiliar garments. Their cut and decorations allow for less freedom of movement than the practical clothes of a soldier. Courtly, formal shoes and the newly brushed hat mentioned in lines 38–39 offer plenty of scope for grotesque deportment from the actor playing Benedick. Don Pedro and Claudio can increase their mockery by pulling or pointing to various items of clothing as they inspect Benedick. Their forensic anatomy offers a comic gender inversion of the usual blazoning of women.

40–62   The men home in to expose Benedick's face and lack of facial hair by forcing his hand away or removing the handkerchief or scarf used as a covering. Their vulture-like fun can be emphasised if they pull away swabs to cover the cuts he has made while shaving himself, thus revealing that he has sold his hair to the barber's man 'to stuff tennis balls', presumably in order to help pay for his expensive new clothes (III.ii.40–45). Getting close to Benedick also allows the characters to sniff as they note that Benedick has washed and is wearing civet as a perfume, prompting a delighted mockery more characteristic of adolescent boys than mature men. Throughout this anatomisation, Benedick remains silent. The actor can register physical discomfort and shame to point up Benedick's insecurity, or endure the torments with a bored patience that suggests the self-confidence and greater maturity which the character shows later in the church scene. Both options, or a mixture of the two, are valid in performance and both reflect Benedick's courage in standing as the butt of his friends' laughter in his new identity as lover. A higher-status Benedick need not necessarily be less funny since he must continually try to overcome a fresh assault or jibe in an attempt to keep face.

63–71 The bawdy suggestion that Beatrice will 'die' (reach orgasm) with her face upwards (under Benedick's body) finally does produce a reaction, as Benedick chivalrously intervenes to protect her, the new target, from mockery. He makes a deliberate move, leading Leonato offstage, away from Don Pedro and Claudio with what appears to be a high-status dismissal of them as 'hobby horses' or clownish boys too immature to appreciate the 'wise words' of marriage negotiations (III.ii.64–66).

Enter* [DON] JOHN *the bastard. Left alone onstage after this interval of merriment, Don Pedro and Claudio must confront their imminent parting. Their comments about what is going on offstage can be played as a way to avoid a potentially emotional and embarrassing private farewell. There may be a short pause or silence to mark this before the entrance of Don John, who has the perfect timing typical of a villain.

72–96 Don John is forced to adopt an uncharacteristic attitude of friendliness towards his brother and Claudio in order to make them believe that his concern for their honour has motivated the revelation about Hero. His greeting should be fulsome, even if it is uttered between metaphorically gritted teeth. Don Pedro probably welcomes this intervention; the fact that he does not notice anything unusual may be a mark of his preoccupation with saying goodbye to Claudio. Don John's apparent reluctance to reveal his news in public is primarily motivated by the danger of his accusation being overheard by anyone else passing through the space – he may look around – but it also has the useful effect of increasing the curiosity of Claudio and Don Pedro. Don John's opening question provokes what is probably an impatient retort from Don Pedro, which Don John responds to cleverly by offering his own observations in a chillingly calm way. He preempts their suspicion by reverting to his usual taciturn manner to increase their wish to hear and swallow the story about Hero.

97–122 Claudio's question 'Disloyal?' may well be aggressive, but Don John retains his composure, and accusation, possibly helped by Don Pedro's use of a hand to restrain Claudio from physical violence. Don John's recommendation that they suspend their 'wonder' and 'bear it coldly' or temperately until they have proper 'warrant' or evidence, makes him appear reasonable. His determination to

'disparage her no farther till you are my witnesses' invisibly shifts responsibility for the tragic disruption of the wedding onto them (III.ii.100 and
116–17). A sinister new trio of male companions is forged through the
repeated apostrophe 'O' in the final exclamations of the scene, before
Don John leads them off in what could be played as a hissingly malicious
and triumphant exit given the 's' alliteration in his final line.

Act III, scene iii

A change of scene is now required as the action moves outside
Leonato's household into the streets of Messina. A bench is required
for the Watch to sit on and a 'penthouse' or porch under which
Borachio and Conrade can shelter from the rain, but otherwise the
stage should be clear to allow Dogberry maximum freedom of movement to march officiously up and down. The public nature of this
space can be economically suggested in a proscenium arch theatre
by playing it downstage while the orchard scene is changed behind
flats or curtains. In a more open stage space like the Globe, the swift
removal of token bushes or branches from one side of the stage is
easily covered by business accompanying the entrance of Dogberry,
Verges, and the members of the Watch who line up to present themselves and their equipment (bills or weapons) for inspection. Since
this is night time and Dogberry is carrying what appears to be the
only lantern, stage business suggesting confusion in the dark is
appropriate. It can set up the forces of the law as comic rather than
fearful. Members of the Watch are drawn from the local community
rather than being professionals in uniform, and could be costumed
with a motley range of hats and cloaks or coats to keep warm. They
may not be used to handling their bills, which belong to the town
armoury and must be carefully watched (III.iii.41).

1–24 Any physical confusion among members of the Watch is
immediately surpassed by Dogberry and Verges's verbal performance. Their confident misuse of language should shock the ears of
spectators who have enjoyed such a fine display of wit in the previous scenes. The ears of modern audiences are generally much less
well attuned than their early modern counterparts to appreciate the
comedy of these exchanges, so additional visual gags can be useful
to sustain the comedy. Dogberry's self-importance and officious

(though genial) air can be embodied effectively by a well-rounded (or padded) actor. A large gown (Dogberry boasts two IV.ii.86–87), swung flamboyantly as he moves down the line of watchmen, may help to convey Dogberry's pomposity. Dogberry's language melds binary opposites through malapropism in a carnivalesque amalgamation of order in disorder and vice versa. He thus prepares, through comedy, for the tragic inversions of the wedding scene, including Claudio's violent defamation of his bride as 'pure impiety and impious purity' (IV.i.104). Dogberry appoints Seacoal presumably because his dark skin or 'favour' makes him the 'most desertless' and 'senseless and fit' man to lead the night duty, jokes which can be pointed up with appropriate, earnest emphasis, and accompanied by a solemn handing over of the lantern to Seacoal.

25–71 Dogberry's subsequent ridiculous advice on how to avoid trouble rather than arrest troublemakers may produce some non-verbal reaction (raising of eyebrows, puzzled scratching of heads) from the Watch. The watchman who declares he will rather sleep than talk since they 'know what belongs to a watch' matches Dogberry at his own game, either subversively or by simply reproducing Dogberry's own speech patterns (III.iii.37–38). Deformation of language appears to be infectious, floating freely in the misreportings which flourish in Messina, and ultimately no more controllable than the mysterious 'deformed thief' fashion that the Watch later mistake as the villain of the piece. Slowing the pace down to spell out the jokes kills them. One solution is to have Dogberry place formal emphasis on selected malapropisms as part of his earnest counsel to the Watch. The actor may be helped by a staff of office which Dogberry uses to literally point out his meaning to the watchmen. Another is to supplement and mark the character's verbal indiscretions with eccentric movement and gestures. Having Dogberry walk up and down the line of watchmen, followed by Verges, offers scope for physical comedy as he is forced to make abrupt stops in his orderly progress, turning back to respond to queries like 'How if they will not stand' and 'If we know him to be a thief, shall we not lay hands on him?' (III.iii.44 and 53–54).

72–84 The dynamic between Dogberry and Verges can draw attention to the former's mistakes. In response to the query about arresting a thief, for example, Dogberry's carefully reasoned but utterly stupid dismissal of the idea is reconfigured as 'mercy' by Verges (III.iii.60). An actor of smaller or slighter stature for this role materialises the idea that he is Dogberry's faithful shadow. When an awkward difference emerges between them on the question of whether Seacoal has the right to stop the Prince himself, Dogberry's rhetorical meanderings create a roundabout way of preserving his status while maintaining the proper respect for superiors, the ideology which governs everything Verges does (III.iii.72–80).

85–91 Since Dogberry has given the lantern to Seacoal, he may have some difficulty trying to exit through the dark, 'Come neighbour' being a covert appeal for a helpful arm to guide him. When Seacoal moves into Dogberry's role, he may imitate the Constable's pompous stance and voice in the direction 'Well, masters, we hear our charge', before recommending they sit down and then go to bed early since it has begun to rain (III.iii.101). Dogberry's surprise return brings them abruptly back to order but does not raise confidence in their ability to apprehend the villains. For the second exit, Verges may light a taper from Seacoal's lantern to guide them, or take the lantern away, thus setting up the Watch to fail. The Watch then move to the bench, either at the side of the stage or upstage. If the first part of the scene is played on the forestage, this can be a cue for the Watch to move upstage (and reopen curtains if necessary). The paradox of the sleeping Watch can be emphasised if they take trouble to arrange themselves comfortably on, beside or behind the bench for sleep rather than vigilance. In a modern design, umbrellas may be raised to offer shelter from the drizzle. If they still have the lantern, it should be ostentatiously blown out.

92–134 Borachio and Conrade enter hurriedly without lights and thus do not notice the darkened Watch. Seacoal could sit upright and lean forward to hear, quietening his colleagues with a hand as they do the same. Borachio has been wooing Margaret as a 'ruffian' so his dress should be rough and unkempt, thus adding irony to his discussion of fashion (III.iii.113–37). The effects of drink (III.iii.101) explain his digression and a loud delivery of lines which the Watch cannot fail to hear. Borachio and Conrade move to the 'penthouse', an overhanging canopy such as that held up by pillars in the Globe which protected the central area of the stage. The rambling Borachio in the original production probably gestured drunkenly to the paintings on the walls of the tiring house in his lines 'sometimes fashioning them like Pharaoh soldiers in the reechy painting, sometime like the god Bel's priests in the old church window, sometime like the shaven Hercules' (III.iii.129–32). An image of Hercules holding the earth was very likely displayed somewhere in the Globe. In more modern theatres, a canopy suspended from the side of a proscenium arch stage or over a vomitory in a theatre in the round creates a suitable space for Conrade and Borachio to be seen and heard by the audience. The Watch too listen agog – with one or two possibly moving forward in the semi-darkness to hear more clearly – as Borachio tells how he earned a thousand ducats from Don John. Borachio's contempt for the fashion of the upper classes understandably attracts the sympathy of an equally scruffy watchman who knows and remembers 'Deformed' as one who 'has been a vile thief this seven year' (III.iii.121–23). Although this is not literally true, the indirections of the watchman's thought do bring to light a pertinent political point in the 1590s environment of fast-changing fashion. In more modern designs, a contrast in the clothing worn by those inside the house and these men on the streets can make a similar point.

135–73 Conrade, apparently more sensitive to the rain than Borachio, begins to lose patience and urges him to get to the point (III.iii.135–37). Since Borachio's narrative is the only account the audience have of the plot's success and Claudio's intention to shame Hero in the church the next morning, this information must be delivered clearly, even if Borachio is somewhat inebriated. His mention of 'Lady Hero', 'Claudio' and, most importantly 'the prince' undoubtedly attracts the attention of the Watch (III.iii.142–56). Seeing an opportunity at last to make use of their bills in a real incident, they could press forward eagerly to take part in an arrest, with Seacoal gesturing silently to get them ready to move in inconspicuously. Borachio may laugh and/or belch in amusement at the first watchman's command 'We charge you in the prince's name, stand!' since he and Conrade are already standing (III.iii.157). Seacoal directs one of his men to summon Dogberry 'the right master Constable' but seems to be fulfilling his role as substitute admirably well in reproducing Dogberry's habit of rhetorical anarchy: 'We have here recovered the most dangerous piece of lechery that was ever known in the commonwealth' and 'Let us obey you to go with us' (III.iii.159–61 and 169–70). The first watchman's reminders about 'Deformed' (III.iii.162), like Dogberry's verbal style, serves to create synergies between the perversions of language and justice. Borachio's reaction is to joke about the arrest rather than resist it, and he is probably too drunk to realise how easy it would be to talk his way out of it. Conrade may be less sanguine, realising that his master's whole plot is in danger of unravelling.

Act III, scene iv

Nervous excitement animates this intimate, all-female scene which takes place in Leonato's house at five o'clock on the wedding morning. Since Hero is urged to 'withdraw' and dress at the imminent arrival of the men, the room is a public space of some kind, though productions often set the scene in Hero's bedroom. Strictly speaking, since Margaret and Hero can carry on the rebato and gloves, nothing is required onstage although a seat of some kind is useful for Hero and for Beatrice to rest on, and to suggest the inside location, while larger items of Hero's wedding attire can be hung over this if desired (see below). In the original production, this 'dressing' scene would have given the four boy actors in the company a rare opportunity to rehearse in public the material construction of a woman which they undertook every time they got ready to perform. Margaret enters already dressed and carrying Hero's rebato or wired collar, while Hero is still wearing just her smock: the garment worn under the assorted petticoats, kirtles, gowns, bodices and sleeves that make up a woman's dress. Since smocks were also used as nightwear and the word was used as a slang term for a sexually loose woman, Hero's entrance in her underwear implicitly sets her up as an easy target for Don John's allegations.

1–21 Margaret's suggestion that the Duchess of Milan's wedding dress is 'but a night-gown in respect of yours' may be a slip that reflects her guilt at having 'borrowed' Hero's dress to wear at the window for her night-time assignation with Borachio. Margaret is obviously a fashion victim who is very interested in the clothes of her social superiors, as seen in her detailed description of the Duchess of Milan's wedding gown with 'cloth o' gold, and cuts, and laced with silver, set with pearls, down sleeves, side sleeves and skirts round underborne with a bluish tinsel' (III.iv.18–20). In the opening section of the scene (III.iv.1–34) she comments on the rebato, Hero's wedding gown, her headdress or 'tire' which is in the neighbouring room, and which she may have tried on herself since she wishes the hair was 'a thought browner' (III.iii.12–13), perhaps to match her own.

If a production chooses to have Hero's wedding dress onstage as a focus for Margaret's speech, the actor can show Margaret's attraction to clothes and dressing up by means of some business: stroking the fabric or even picking the dress up and holding it against herself to suggest a Margaret who is really cheeky. Playing with the wedding dress makes clear that it is a 'mobile' sartorial signifier which could recreate the servant Margaret as the Lady Hero, as well as being passed from one boy actor to another in early modern revivals as the production moved from public theatres to the Court. Keeping the dress offstage in this scene increases the sense of spectacle when the actor appears as the bride in Act IV scene i. Margaret is tactless and Hero, already nervous about the day ahead, may show impatience with Margaret's criticisms of her choice of accessories and the comparison of her wedding dress to the Duchess of Milan's.

22–34 If the wedding dress is onstage, Hero can lift it from the seat and sit down with it to show her low mood on the line 'God give me joy to wear it, for my heart is exceeding heavy' (III.iv.22–23). As a servant, Margaret should have a job in this scene; combing her mistress's hair before the rebato and tire are affixed is the first logical stage in dressing, so it is probably here, when Hero sits down, that Margaret goes to the back of the chair and begins this task. She tries to jolly her mistress along with a bawdy joke about the 'weight of a man' on the wedding night, and defends her indelicate humour with pious reference to St Paul's idea that love between a man and woman in marriage is honourable (Heb. 13:4 see p. 94). Such teasing may irritate Hero even further and can be telegraphed by the actor grimacing or putting up her hand to stop Margaret's coiffure.

35–86 Beatrice's entrance creates a diversion, particularly since her sharp wit is now muffled by a cold, which can be indicated by sneezes and the use of a handkerchief. Some productions provide a reason for the cold by having Beatrice get wet during the overhearing scene (if, for example, Hero and Ursula are occupied with watering plants in the orchard and deliberately drench her). No explanation is necessary though; the point of the cold is to make Beatrice vulnerable rather than sharp-tongued like Margaret in this scene. Hero is probably quite relieved to shift attention to her cousin, to whom she expresses concern: getting up to put an arm round Beatrice on 'Why, how now? Dost thou speak in the sick tune?' and sitting Beatrice down on the chair in her place. Beatrice manages to parry Margaret's joking request that she sing 'Light o' love' with the suggestion that Margaret's wantonness will produce many bastard children for her husband (III.iv.40–45). It is to support Hero that Beatrice has come, however, in spite of feeling 'exceeding ill'. She may get up and take the brush or comb from Margaret and summon Hero with the reminder ''Tis almost five o' clock, cousin; 'tis time you were ready' (III.iv.47–48). This is, of course, an implicit reprimand of Margaret for talking rather than getting on with her work. Rather than being annoyed with Margaret's self-importance, however, Beatrice is simply too tired or ill to bandy words with her. Margaret's curiosity about how Beatrice has responded to the news about Benedick probably prompts her teasing mention of *carduus benedictus* as a good cure for a cold (III.iv.71–85).

87–91   The joke appears to have lifted Hero's sense of melancholy by the time Ursula, in her role as housekeeper, runs on with news of the arrival of Claudio, Don Pedro and the 'gallants of the town' to conduct Hero to the church. Her excitement and panic in the last line 'Help to dress me, good coz, good Meg, good Ursula' unites the four women in a shared, swift exit (III.iv.87–91).

Act III, scene v

1–15   This scene, which may be in the same room or at the doorway to Leonato's house, holds out a final opportunity to prevent the disaster in the church, as Dogberry and Verges arrive to convey their news. Dogberry's pride in announcing the arrest of 'two a[u]spicious persons' (III.v.44) to the Governor of Messina can be conveyed through costume, tone and stance. The Constable should be dressed impeccably as befits the occasion: in his gown and carrying his staff of office. A ceremony of hat removal and series of bows could be used to demonstrate his determination to make the most of this occasion, and create a comic contrast with Leonato's impatience to leave the house.

16–49 Dogberry and Verges's circumlocutions ultimately provoke Leonato's unequivocal 'Neighbours, you are tedious'. A smile and bow can show that Dogberry mistakes this as a compliment, as he generously offers to bestow 'all his tediousness' on Leonato (III. v.17–22). Comedy barely diffuses the audience's frustration when Dogberry refuses to let Verges speak, perhaps physically moving between him and Leonato with a lengthy, patronising apology which prevents the news reaching him (III.v.32–39). Leonato's invitation to 'drink some wine before you go' (III.v.49) in order to offset his rather brusque treatment of them can be greeted with vigorous nods and elaborate expressions of thanks.

50–60 The messenger's arrival finally gives Leonato the escape route he needs. After their hurried exit, there may be a pause while Dogberry and Verges look around expectantly for the drinks and are disappointed. With perhaps a sigh and a glance at a clock, watch or the sun, the tedious Constable determines that, as a man on important civic business, he cannot, regretfully, waste any more time, and dismisses his deputy to make arrangements for the examination of the prisoners.

Act IV

Act IV, scene i

This is the dramatic climax of the play with both plots coming to a head: Claudio's denunciation of Hero as the result of Don John's determination to destroy the match; and Beatrice and Benedick's first encounter following Don Pedro's orchestration of the overhearing plots. The scene juxtaposes elements of violence, despair, tragedy, tenderness and romance to create an emotional rollercoaster for characters and spectators. The church setting need not be elaborate: the presence of a suitably accoutred Friar will invoke the solemnity required. A simple table to serve as an altar and a cross placed on it help to recreate the sense of a sacred space onstage, and thus increase the significance of Claudio's desecration of the wedding ceremony. Further small items that typically feature in traditional Western weddings such as candles, floral decorations and ribbons, chairs for the congregation, can be employed to build up audience engagement with what is staged. The familiarity of these elements from spectators' own direct or indirect experiences of weddings helps to create an atmosphere in which the solemnity of the occasion in early modern England translates into the present onstage and off, engaging spectators as participants like members of the congregation. Lighting with a gobo to create the impression of a stained glass window can effectively convey the size of the church, suggesting to performers and spectators that this is a public arena, unlike Leonato's house.

Enter DON PEDRO, [DON JOHN *the*] *bastard,* LEONATO, FRIAR, CLAUDIO, BENEDICK, HERO *and* BEATRICE [*with others*]   One effective way to establish the ceremonial occasion is to begin with formal entries: first of Friar Francis to his place in front of the altar, if there is one, and then a procession of the bridal party into their positions following the conventional blocking for a wedding ceremony in which the bride, as the left rib of Adam, is placed on the left of the groom. This might be accompanied by music suitable for setting the tone of a ceremony that is 'full of state and ancientry' as Beatrice said (II.i.68). Entries through the auditorium will implicitly construct the audience as members of the congregation. In addition to Claudio, Don Pedro, Don John and Benedick, who position themselves stage left, with Antonio and Balthasar if there are sufficient actors to create a more public occasion. Solemn but determined looks (with a smug or celebratory, villainous smile from Don John) serve to maintain the orderly letter of the service even though they are about to destroy it. In an early modern design, the men should be dressed in formal courtly costume with gloves (which were given as gifts to both male and female guests at early modern weddings). For productions set in later periods, the option of costuming Don Pedro's party in dress military uniform signals a withdrawal back to the aggressive all-male world of the battlefield. Benedick, who has just turned lover and is ignorant of what is about to happen, can be costumed differently in order to signal his wish to impress Beatrice and to forecast his break from the all-male group. His first glance, having found his correct place, could be across to Beatrice.

If the production chooses to mimic contemporary wedding traditions, Leonato and Hero will enter after the groom's party, followed by Beatrice and, if resources allow, Ursula and Margaret (who, if onstage, should react to the news of Hero's supposed encounter at her window). The bride's party moves up stage right. Like the other men, Leonato should be wearing formal dress of some kind and gloves. Early modern wedding dresses were not traditionally white but Hero's costume should, even when not white, make her the centre of the stage spectacle. The gloves Claudio gave her, the rebato (high, wired collar) and the 'tire' or headdress discussed in Act III scene iv should feature. A wedding headdress and veil could be substituted for these items if it is not an early modern design. Hero's costume and bouquet of flowers should suggest her purity. Claudio tells her 'You seem to me as Dian in her orb' and, for these lines to work, her appearance must make a dramatic contrast to the 'savage sensuality' he believes lies beneath. Beatrice can take the role of bridesmaid which dates back to early modern practices, and receive Hero's flowers when she steps up to be married. Given Beatrice's bad cold, she may have an extra shawl and handkerchiefs. If she sneezes, Benedick could express concern and she embarrassment. There should be signs of a high level of excitement and emotion from the protagonists now that the moment has finally arrived. The lines suggest that Leonato is particularly nervous.

Dogberry, Verges and Members of the Watch, who are from a different social class, are busy at the prisoners' examination and so not present. Some productions make use of supernumeraries as additional guests or clerical attendants. The presence of so many bodies onstage has the useful effect of increasing the impact of Claudio's public shaming of Hero and the need to publish her innocence to 'the people of Messina' (V.i.271). It should not, however, block any sightlines to the protagonists who are the focus of the scene. As noted above, some auditoria and productions can effectively co-opt the audience as members of a congregation.

1–21   The words beginning the wedding scene invite the early modern audience in as witnesses to the ceremony. Leonato specifies it will be the 'plain form of marriage' (IV.i.1): the service in the *Book of Common Prayer* (1558) in which the congregation provided an authorising witness to the bride and groom's enactment of the rite. The recitation of the opening words of the service (lines 4–12) has the effect of invoking the solemnity of the church ceremony and heightening its abuse by Claudio. The first interruption to the ceremony is misinterpreted as an objection to the form of service. Claudio's answer 'No' to the Friar's opening question 'You come hither, my lord, to marry this lady' will probably cause a reaction – shown by sharp intakes of breath, puzzled looks among the bride's party and guests. Leonato interrupts, exhibiting an anxiety to move on in his line 'To be married to her, Friar, you come to marry her' (IV.i.6). While the older matrimonial rites gave emphasis to the priest's role in sprinkling rings with holy water, blessing them and ratifying the marriage, in the solemnisation of matrimony found in the *Book of Common Prayer* the bride and groom effectively married themselves: 'the two actually taking each other to be man and wife, and testifying the same with express words and by mutual pledges' as William Gouge put it (Gouge, 1622, 205). The minister's job was to proclaim they were married since they 'have consented together in holy wedlock and have witnessed the same before God and this company' rather than to marry them (cited in Cressy, 1997, 341). Leonato interprets Claudio's 'No' as a wish to return to the more traditional form and his line may get a nervous laugh from the assembled onstage audience. What spectators witness is Claudio's refusal to marry himself to Hero. Leonato's haste here and when Claudio is asked to declare any impediment to the marriage gives Claudio no chance to state his objections in an orderly way. He may pause, perhaps mustering his courage to speak, and Leonato (again anxious to fill the tense silence) declares: 'I dare make his answer: none' (IV.i.16). Claudio appears to lose his control momentarily and Benedick, unable to understand what is going on, can take a step forward and intervene in an attempt to excuse Claudio's embarrassing 'interjections' as a rush of blood to the head, to be dismissed as an eccentric sense of humour (IV.i.19–20).

21–43 Claudio's next move is critical: in asking the Friar to stand aside and taking his position centre stage, Claudio makes clear his refusal to continue with the wedding. Before Hero or Leonato have time to say anything, he initiates a desecrated form of the ceremony presided over by himself, first inviting Leonato to give Hero to him. The formality of gesture is important, being the only script with which an increasingly anxious congregation of characters and off-stage spectators is familiar in this strange atmosphere. Leonato hands Hero over to Claudio as his 'son' according to convention. Claudio, equally formally, takes Hero's hand as though weighing her worth while he prominently displays her to the congregation, asking what can he give back to Leonato to match such a 'rich and precious gift'. This time Leonato dare not answer to fill the silence and it is the high-status voice of Don Pedro which effectively authorises this anti-wedding with the words 'Nothing unless you render her again' (IV.i.25–27). This line and Claudio's 'Sweet Prince, you learn me noble thankfulness' are chillingly calm before Claudio passes his bride back to her father as a 'rotten orange'. If spoken quietly this coldly objective assessment of Hero's worth can, ironically, make Claudio appear even more callous and unsympathetic than an explosion of anger in which he physically pushes or throws his bride back to her father. Hero's signs of shock and shame at being treated thus produce the fatal blush that drives Claudio to distraction. Most actors cannot blush on demand, making the blush the creation of Shakespeare's text and Claudio's imagination (which the audience may or may not share). He speaks as though unable to comprehend the discrepancy between the 'sign and semblance' of beauty that he sees and what he now believes she is: a wanton. Beatrice can come forward to put an arm round her cousin, occupying them both with stage business such as rearranging Hero's headdress or giving her back her flowers while Leonato speaks.

44–60 Leonato shows signs of desperation here: still trying to rescue the wedding which he has anticipated for so many years, he concludes there has been an excusable premarital assignation between the lovers and may move quickly towards Claudio in an attempt to deal with this privately (IV.i.44–46). Claudio interrupts him – perhaps with an outstretched hand which stops him in his tracks. Hero recovers herself sufficiently to speak up in her own defence; she might speak somewhat angrily (IV.i.54). She is totally unprepared for Claudio's violent reaction: 'Out on thee, seeming!' If Claudio is to be at all sympathetic, the actor needs to convey something of the character's pain as well as his anger in the following lines about Hero, the perfect bride, appearing 'as Dian in her orb / As chaste as is the bud ere it be blown' (IV.i.56–7). The dazzling spectacle she presents is one of enchanting purity. She can stand perfectly still, perhaps holding her bouquet of flowers: the absolute antithesis of 'Venus or those pampered animals / That rage in savage sensuality' (IV.i.59–60).

61–68   A good parallel study for the actor playing Claudio is Troilus, who can only exclaim 'This is, and is not, Cressid!' when confronted with evidence of his mistress's infidelity (*Troilus and Cressida*, V.ii.146). The bifurcation of Hero into a superficial illusion of divine chastity and an embodiment of sexual licentiousness is captured in his exclamations 'Hero itself can blot out Hero's virtue' (IV.i.82) and 'O Hero! what a Hero had'st thou been' if her 'outward graces' had been matched by her behaviour. Claudio's farewell to the beautiful figure in front of him is a highly tortured form of rhetorical wit, laced with paradox: 'fare thee well, most foul, most fair. Farewell / Thou pure impiety and impious purity' (IV.i.100–104). If these lines are spoken with an eye on his own elegant, controlled, performance, Claudio will appear as an utterly self-centred figure with no real feeling for Hero. For a more sympathetic Claudio, these are lines of passion from a man who finds it very painful and difficult to tear himself away from what looks like a material embodiment of his ideal woman.

Hero, Leonato and Benedick's expressions can supplement their words of disbelief at what Claudio pronounces. Hero quickly wonders – perhaps leaning or moving forward in a mixture of concern and challenge – 'Is my lord well that he doth speak so wide?' (IV. i.61). Leonato likewise doubts Claudio's judgement and makes a turn to appeal to Don Pedro who can step forward on Claudio's side of the church (stage left) to give his testimony, followed by Don John (IV.i.62–66). The shadowing of the 'good' brother by his 'villainous' bastard other should be apparent here. Hero's reaction 'True? Oh God!' can be preceded by a searching look at Claudio who remains steadfast. Benedick then has time to quickly interject 'This looks not like a nuptial' before Hero speaks (IV.i.67–68). This is the cue for any supernumeraries to make a hasty, embarrassed exit.

69–109   As Benedick's line indicates, the mode of the scene now changes from a sacred ceremony to a courtroom interrogation, paralleling the one happening offstage under Dogberry's direction. The church setting makes it a kind of 'catechizing' as Hero is put on trial (IV.i.78). The Friar may take a step forward to oversee what is going on. She is first called to answer to her name (IV.i.79), then to answer the prosecutory accusation (IV.i.84–85) and hear the evidence of Don Pedro as witness (IV.i.87–94), corroborated with abstract hyperbole by Don John (IV.i.95–99). If Margaret is onstage during this scene, she gradually realises her own responsibility for what has happened as Claudio and Don Pedro give details of the night-time encounter. The actor can register this with a look of dawning horror, and when she looks around for Borachio, of course, he is not there. She is either too afraid or too ashamed to speak up and may bury her face in her hands or slip offstage, out of the church. The courtroom atmosphere fixes all the other characters rigidly into their positions, leaving Hero exposed as a very different kind of spectacle from that which she imagined earlier that morning. Her faint, which should be sudden and shocking, may be the result of the whole traumatic experience, culminating in Claudio's farewell speech, or perhaps prompted more immediately by her father's line 'Hath no man's dagger here a point for me?' (IV.i.109), which signals his belief in the story rather than in her. Her faint ends the trial and Don Pedro, Claudio and Don John, assuming it is proof of their accusations (IV.i.112), exit as a group. The exit may not be uniform, hesitation reflecting concern or guilt by a more sympathetic Claudio or Don Pedro, in contrast to Don John. Alternatively, a group exit without a backward glance points up the cruelty of their behaviour. Benedick, significantly, does not follow them.

110–20 Hero's collapse breaks up the courtroom's cold formality, and Beatrice can rush forward to pick up her cousin's fallen form and stoutly reassert her innocence with the words 'Wherefore sink you down?' (IV.i.110). None of the men follows Beatrice. If a maternal Ursula rushes to Hero's side, a gendered division is created by the blocking of this moment. Benedick may take a step forward after Don Pedro, but his line and gaze focus on the body of Hero and he remains behind to ask 'How doth the lady?' (IV.i.113). Beatrice, fearing the worst, appeals to each of the men in turn. 'Help, uncle! ... Uncle, Signor Benedick, Friar!' (IV.i.114). Pauses – even very short ones – can highlight the lack of male help. When Leonato does not move, refusing – or unable – to recognise his daughter because of what he has heard, Father Francis responds *in loco parentis*, perhaps kneeling down to examine Hero's body. The substitution continues through the following lines with the spiritual Father offering encouragement: 'Have comfort, lady' in opposition to Leonato's accusatory 'Dost thou look up?'; then defending Hero with 'Yes, wherefore should she not?' (IV.i.118–19).

120–44   It is Friar Francis who protects the prostrate Hero in the face of her father Leonato's damning attack: 'doth not every earthly thing / Cry shame upon her?' and 'Do not live, Hero, do not ope thine eyes!' (IV.i.120–23). The actor's interpretation of these lines to suggest pain as well as anger is crucial to retaining a degree of understanding if not sympathy from spectators. This is especially so for many modern audiences, to whom Leonato's extremely possessive paternal attitude will be alien. The violence of his feelings towards Hero includes a wish to 'strike at thy life' that is born of the same passion as Claudio's earlier pain at the destruction of an ideal. Like Claudio, he asks 'Why wast thou ever lovely in my eyes?' (IV.i.130). The lines are not logical; Leonato has no reason to think that Hero is anything but the chaste daughter he believed in, but the shame at apparently failing in his paternal task may combine with the inevitable build-up of emotions at the wedding to produce his outrageously self-centred outburst. Leonato's speech (IV.i.120–43) has 24 references to himself, the most extreme concentration in his view of Hero as 'mine, and mine I loved, and mine I praised / And mine that I was proud on'. His pronouns give a keen sense of how his only child has been the exclusive focus of his emotional attention 'mine so much / That I myself was to myself not mine / Valuing of her' (IV.i.136–39). The possessive force conveyed here suggests that the trauma of losing Hero to another man in marriage may be bound up with Leonato's expressions of outrage at his daughter.

143–45   Benedick probably assumes it would be inappropriate for him, a stranger, to touch Hero, though he can move closer to her and to Beatrice, showing concern by expressions of relief to see her stir and to hear the Friar speak to her. Benedick's chivalric intervention to stop Leonato defaming his daughter as 'foul-tainted flesh' serves to protect them and the listeners from further shame. Benedick remains neutral; in his own words 'so attired in wonder / I know not what to say'.

146–54   Beatrice immediately challenges him to defend Hero's innocence ('O, on my soul my cousin is belied!'), probably standing up to do so (IV.i.143–46). This is the first time the two have spoken since the overhearing scenes and their dialogue (which must involve direct, extended eye contact) is remarkably selfless and matter-of-fact: their primary concern is to help Hero. Benedick sensibly attempts to examine the evidence. Beatrice is angry that, for this one night, she did not sleep in the same room as Hero, though she can undermine Don Pedro's ridiculous fantasy of Hero meeting with a lover 'a thousand times in secret' (IV.i.94) because of her past experience, and probably speaks with some vehemence. She can then return to look after Hero, the exchange having established a sense of understanding or alliance between Beatrice and Benedick, which is all the more important in the face of Leonato's despairing belief in Don Pedro and Claudio (IV.i.150–54).

155–75 The Friar's intervention adds a second, more powerful patriarchal authority to the counsel for Hero's defence. Once he has given primary care of Hero back to Beatrice (and possibly Ursula), Leonato's lines give the Friar a motive to stand quietly centre stage at the altar and offer his own advice. The actor playing this role needs to speak firmly and calmly; his wisdom is like that of Solomon. His voice restores faith in Hero and his judgement is based on rational evidence from his 'noting of the lady' (IV.i.158) as well as his reverence and experience. He cleverly asks Hero to name her supposed lover, who has so far remained anonymous, and her inability to do so corroborates her innocence. Independence from worldly power gives the Friar licence to suggest the princes are mistaken, a responsibility he can assume with gravity.

177–200 Hero may gather strength from the Friar and, in response to his question, can stand to assert 'They know that do accuse me. I know none' (IV.i.176–77). Turning to refute her father's accusation, and challenging him to 'prove' the charge before he tortures her to death, can be played as a further step in strength and outrage, or as something which she finds very difficult to face. Benedick remains calm, possibly speaking from his side of the church (stage left) to defend his friends by testifying that Don John is the likely culprit. By contrast, Leonato is possessed by passion: he wishes to commit violence on either Hero or her wrongers.

200–54 The Friar's stage presence must be strong to give force to his restraining order 'Pause awhile' before he relates his plan. Everyone onstage must be drawn into the scheme, giving him their undivided attention. Benedick uses his male authority to recommend acceptance of the plan in words, while Beatrice can nod silently, pointing up the fact that her female voice has no legitimacy. Leonato's sudden vulnerability – 'the smallest twine may lead me' (IV.i.249–50) – can be shown in signs of grief and exhaustion as he submits to the Friar's guidance in physical as well as strategic terms. The Friar's quiet authority is encapsulated in the way his quatrain closes the public part of the scene. An exit where Leonato and Hero take each other's arms to follow the Friar pathetically repeats their entrance to the church, and telegraphs a sense of reconciliation between father and daughter in the hope 'this wedding day / Perhaps is but prolonged' (IV.i.253–54).

255–66 Hero's exit allows Beatrice to show the extent of her grief in the privacy of the near-deserted church. There must be a pause before Benedick comes forward to ask 'Lady Beatrice, have you wept all this while?' (IV.i.255), a question which expresses concern since the answer is obvious. She can put her face back into her hands, or turn away to resume crying, to prompt his assertion 'your fair cousin is wronged' (IV.i.260): the only way he can think of to offer support. Even though this was probably not his primary intention, the remark does distract her from her private sorrow, and onto a more active response. The actor playing Beatrice must decide whether she is already thinking of killing Claudio when she says 'How much might the man deserve of me that would right her', If so, she may not yet have identified Benedick as a possible instrument for her revenge. The actor playing Benedick has a single focus: professing his friendship to Beatrice rather than thinking of any possible consequences.

267–86 A silence can follow 'not yours' (IV.i.266), before he plucks up the courage to tell Beatrice 'I do love nothing in the world so well as you'. The church setting gives these words a resonance that they would not have elsewhere (perhaps literally so if there is an echo). It is, as he acknowledges, a 'strange' moment to declare his love, and she can show that she does not expect it through silence and her delivery of the following lines. Most unusually, Beatrice does not know what to say. Using the rhetoric of church and court, she makes a confession of her love to him but it is hedged with confusion: 'believe me not – and yet I lie not. I confess nothing; nor yet deny nothing'. The only thing she can say without equivocation is 'I am sorry for my cousin' (IV.i.270–72). The following exchange and the idea of swearing by the sword pushes Benedick to swear his integrity and Beatrice to protest the extent of her love. Her admission 'I love you with so much of my heart that none is left to protest' is a naked exposure of her feelings that can be marked by a change of pace, tone and volume to distinguish it from the parry of wits that has ruled their exchanges to date.

287–99 The dramatic climax of the following lines needs careful preparation by the actors with a view to possible reactions from the audience since 'Kill Claudio' sometimes produces surprised laughter. Benedick's line 'Come, bid me do anything for thee' can be played as a mixture of joy, triumph, affection, and bravado and accompanied by an equally expansive, gesture – opening his arms for example. Beatrice's challenge 'Kill Claudio' hits him with almost physical force. His spontaneous reaction 'Ha, not for the wide world' can carry any audience laughter while simultaneously registering his shock (IV.i.287–89).

It is less clear that Beatrice's ultimatum occurs spontaneously. She may feel the risk of another betrayal by Benedick and the need to test whether he will eat his words, right back to his first strange declaration of love at line 270. However, the challenge may be a spontaneous reaction to his offer, expressing honestly her heart's desire to kill Claudio, and it may surprise her too. In this interpretation, only after she has spoken the challenge does she realise that it is a test of his love, of whether she has risked her whole heart again for nothing. In either case, the line is deadly serious. Benedick's initial refusal confirms Beatrice's worst fears that 'there is no love in you' (IV.i.292). Ashamed and angry at having been so foolish as to give her heart for false dice again, she is desperate to get away from Benedick and can show this physically by pulling away with some force when he prevents her exit. From her perspective, 'Tarry, sweet Beatrice' (IV.i.291) may sound like a cruel attempt to tease her further. For Benedick, however, this is an equally desperate attempt to explain his spontaneous throw-away remark and convince her that there *is* love in him. In whatever physical contact is staged here, the actors have an opportunity to show that the characters are still in conflict in spite of their declarations of love. Instead of a lovers' embrace, Shakespeare stages a struggle. Beatrice asserts 'I am gone, though I am here', and objects 'nay, I pray you, let me go', while Benedick insists 'we'll be friends first' (IV.i.291–96) – perhaps interposing himself between her and the exit in an attempt to heal the breach between them. What follows is an opportunity for Beatrice to restate the terms of the challenge, spelling out its significance in terms of loyalty, and for Benedick to reconsider his response.

300–21   A Beatrice who feels wounded again by Benedick might express her personal bitterness via her attacks on Claudio, who has dishonoured and hurt her kinswoman at the altar. The power of her passion for revenge is made tangible in her wish to 'eat his heart in the market place' (IV.i.305) and bubbles over as she thinks of how Hero has been abused. Woven in with her disgust at 'Count Comfit' is a contempt for male insincerity: 'manhood is melted into curtsies' – formal politeness – 'valour into compliment', and, worst of all, 'men are only turned into tongue and trim ones too': they lie (IV.i.314–22). In performance, her anger about Benedick's false vows can be bundled together with rage and fear that these are not a thing of the past but of the present and the future. Her passion drives her speech along; the delivery must allow Benedick no opportunity to intervene. A change of tone or slowing for the final sentence can mark Beatrice's frustration: 'I cannot be a man with wishing, therefore I will die a woman with grieving', before she makes another move to exit.

322–32   Benedick stops her and vows his love again 'by this hand': either proffering it to her or holding it up in testimony. The challenge is then replayed. Slower, more deliberate delivery and movement between the two actors can mark the added solemnity, the references to belief and souls invoking the resonance of the sacred space in which they are standing. Having accepted the challenge, Benedick speaks in short, sharp sentences typical of a soldier: 'I will challenge him' and 'I will kiss your hand and so I leave you' and 'As you hear of me, so think of me', for example (IV.i.328–32). Each of these is loaded with a keen emotional sensitivity, however. Benedick knows exactly what is at stake in the line 'Claudio shall render me a dear account' and acknowledges the pain Hero is suffering too in his words 'Go comfort your cousin'. More than anything, 'so think of me' is weighted with the depth of his love for Beatrice. This understated Benedick has abandoned the trim tongue for the sword and knows how serious the consequences will be. The declaration of love between the two has moved way beyond romance to a pledging of faith. Paradoxically, they leave the church separately, via different exits, yet closer than they have ever been before.

Act IV, scene ii

This scene takes place in the prison, an appropriate setting for the proper procedures of justice, in contrast to the previous scene's tragic miscarriage of justice in the impugning of Hero's chastity, and the equally serious trial of Benedick's love by duel.

1–62 Dogberry's officious opening line 'Is our whole dissembly appeared?' immediately inverts ordered appearances into carnivalesque chaos, however. Comic business might accompany the passing of a stool and cushion right across the line of Watchmen to the Sexton before proceedings can begin. Dogberry's pride in presenting himself and Verges, with swishes of gowns, as 'the malefactors' is slightly deflated when the Sexton waves them aside to see 'the offenders' (IV.ii.4–7). Once invited to 'let them come before, master constable', however, Dogberry's status rises again, in ordering them brought forward to his view and ordering the Sexton what to write, even though the Sexton conducts the examination of witnesses himself. The Sexton's increasing sense of urgency in getting to the heart of the matter is at odds with Dogberry's inflated sense of himself. Nevertheless, Dogberry's status battle with Borachio inadvertently produces glimpses of truth which can be emphasised by Dogberry using his staff of office or finger to make his points. 'Why, this is flat perjury, to call the prince's brother villain' (IV.ii.43–4) is a comment which draws attention to Don John's cardboard villainy, supposedly explained by his bastardy. It is perjury to lay sole blame on Don John's plots since their success relies on a fear of female sexuality and a latent antipathy to marriage held by the all-male group. When Dogberry mislabels Borachio's crime as 'flat burglary' instead of 'perjury' (IV.ii.52) the error reminds spectators of Borachio's role in manipulating Don John for his own mercenary gain. Dogberry's exclamatory conclusion 'thou wilt be condemned into everlasting redemption for this!' (IV.ii.58–9) comically suggests that people do not get what they deserve. This is clear in the case of Hero and can raise questions about the play's neat happy ending.

63–68   Having elicited the incriminating information, the Sexton reveals the news about John's disappearance and Hero's death, which should produce some non-verbal reaction, ranging from remorse to fear, from Borachio and Conrade. The Sexton sees the need for haste in communicating the testimonies to Leonato and exits quickly, leaving behind his stool and cushion.

69–88   The Constables spread their gowns and authority to fill the scene as they give orders for the villains to be bound. The insults of 'coxcomb' and 'ass' are an affront to be exaggerated rather than tolerated. Dogberry rises to the occasion, proving himself an ass as he circles the villains like a pompous schoolteacher talking down to pupils. His lesson might be punctuated by commanding gestures to Borachio and Conrade and to the members of the Watch who are to remember, presumably by watching since it cannot be written down, that he is an ass. Dogberry embodies the arrogance and the inevitable shortcomings of Messina in his self-proclamation as a 'wise fellow' (Don Pedro and Benedick), an 'officer' (Claudio) and a 'householder' (Leonato) who misreads what he sees (IV.ii.81–3). His complacency about having 'two gowns and everything handsome about him' (IV. ii.86–7) strikes a cautionary note about the folly of Messina's obsession with superficial appearances. Since he orders the others offstage, his final line 'O that I had been writ down an ass!' can be effectively shared with the audience, subversively extending the scope of his perverse wisdom beyond the stage to their social worlds.

Act V

Act V, scene i

The play moves faster than the Sexton to the outside of Leonato's house, where the curious exchange between Antonio and his brother about grief gives the initial impression that the two men have forgotten that Hero is not really dead. Since the action takes place later on the day of the broken wedding, it is possible that Don Pedro and Claudio have not yet removed everything from their quarters in Leonato's house, so the scene could take place in the hall or entrance.

1–44 It is clear that Leonato has not received the news of Borachio and Don John's exposure. His relatively calm exit from the church at the end of IV.i has been superseded by a return of his extreme, nervous temperament. He is just as self-obsessed as he was when lamenting the loss of Hero into the pit of inky infamy. His competitive claim that no father 'so loved his child' is measured out in bodily terms: grief takes the form of how far one can reach or how deeply one can groan. It is a virtuoso performance of fatherly grief whose self-reflexivity is the only means to 'fetter strong madness in a silken thread' (V.i.25), to keep a form of control. Antonio's dry rejoinder to his brother's loud protestation of grief is that 'therein do men from children nothing differ'. It is unclear whether the text intends Leonato to be a satiric portrait or whether we are meant to sympathise with his fatherly sense of shame (if not loss) as a tragically disabling experience. It could, of course, be both, as by scornfully noting the ridiculous spectacle he presents, we fail to appreciate the grief within which 'passeth show' (*Hamlet* I.ii.85). Antonio's call for revenge 'Make those that do offend you suffer too' (V.i.40) rouses Leonato to think beyond himself.

44–79 Don Pedro and Claudio enter 'hastily', obviously embarrassed still to be in Messina and possibly even in Leonato's house since he sarcastically bids them 'fare you well'. Claudio's callousness in formally wishing them both 'Good day' on this of all days doubtless inflames Leonato's passion. He is obviously to the fore until Antonio adds a warning threat: 'If he could right himself with quarrelling / Some of us would lie low' (V.i.51). An effective way to stage this would be to have Leonato and Antonio preventing Don Pedro and Claudio's exit from the house. Claudio acts like a soldier, immediately putting his hand to his sword, a reprehensible act indoors, which he attempts to excuse with a lie. There are no stage directions here but Leonato's formal challenge to Claudio (V.i.62–67) could involve the throwing down of a glove, a more decorous form which implicitly critiques Claudio's barbarous attempt to draw his sword in his host's house or close by.

80–108 When Antonio enters the fray with 'He shall kill two of us', this too can involve throwing down one of the gloves previously worn at the wedding: 'Win me and wear me!' (V.i.80–82). A potentially comic reversal occurs as Leonato now tries to restrain his brother. Antonio is outraged by Don Pedro and Claudio's fashionably military clothes (perhaps the very dress uniforms worn for the wedding scene), and insults them as 'fashion-monging boys' who 'Go anticly and show outward hideousness' to disguise their cowardice (V.i.94–97). Such lines are, of course, deliberately provocative. Don Pedro's refusal to rise to their challenge, followed by a repetition of the good grounds of 'proof' on which Hero was charged must be followed by a move-ment across stage away from them. If Leonato and Antonio have left their gloves onstage, they can still exit (further) into the house with the determination to 'be heard' at a later date and the threat that some 'will smart for it' (V.i.107–108).

109–87 *Enter* BENEDICK   Benedick's entrance blocks Don Pedro and Claudio's exit. They expect a jovial discussion; Claudio's greet-ing 'Now, signor, what news?' is made in anticipation of some fun or 'wit' (V.i.124) from Benedick. He pointedly ignores the first comment and addresses Don Pedro, with whom he does not have a quarrel. He undercuts Claudio's wish for witty repartee with the warning that his wit lies 'in my scabbard'. When they tease him 'draw to pleasure us', probably with sexual innuendo, they need to show that they are taken aback by Benedick's 'pale' look. A rigidly straight posture and gritted teeth are one way to convey Benedick's dangerously quiet anger. The only way he can escape the brittle jokiness of his erstwhile friends is to draw Claudio aside to issue the challenge. Audience attention should be directed towards the two of them by Don Pedro's puzzled gaze, followed by his question 'What, a feast, a feast?' (V.i.150). Sensitive to the uncertain mood of nervous 'good cheer' (V.i.149), Don Pedro returns to the subject of Beatrice, and, when even this produces no reaction from Benedick, they hint at the plot to deceive him 'when he was hid in the garden' (V.i.175). Benedick, who has moved well beyond such superficial tokens of romance, patronisingly refers to Claudio as 'Boy' and 'Lord Lackbeard'. Doubtless even more surprising to them, he brushes off the hint of their plot as 'gossip-like humour' (V.i.180–81) rather than picking up the bait. Quiet, calm delivery as he rejects Don Pedro's company with absolute politeness gives him status, which is increased when he reveals the bombshell of Don John's escape and their infamy in denouncing Hero. A dignified, determined exit emphasises his stature.

188–99 Don Pedro and Claudio rightly conclude that Benedick has offered the challenge 'for the love of Beatrice' (V.i.190–91). Their amusement at this – with reassuring slaps of the shoulder – is punctured by Don Pedro's recollection that Don John has fled.

190–220 The invasion of the stage by Dogberry, Verges (and presumably the Watch though they are not mentioned in the quarto) leading Borachio and Conrade 'two of my brother's men' (V.i.204) physically represents the return of trouble, of whatever Don Pedro and Claudio's so-called wisdom has repressed in order to believe Don John's plot. Dogberry's homely image of the goddess Justice weighing raisins in her scales (V.i.200–1) is the first of another series of obfuscations which give Don Pedro the chance for deferring discovery of the truth with jokes. Dogberry and Verges need to show their delight at encountering the Prince himself while in performance of their duties. Dogberry doubtless pays ceremonial respect to his royal patron with a gestural language to rival his verbal style as he lists the offences (stepping forward, removing his hat, bowing, replacing his hat, taking a step back and so on). If so, Don Pedro can parody this by punctuating each item of his verbal response with an answering gesture. This formality accomplished, Don Pedro moves physically past the triumphant Dogberry in order to address Borachio directly.

221–48 Borachio briefly recounts the plot, his tone perhaps raising questions about his profession of remorse. He certainly showed no 'shame' in recounting his villainy before and may even take malicious pleasure in the effect of his story on Claudio. 'The reward of a villain' thus seems justified. Nevertheless, Don Pedro's readiness to shift the burden of villainy to his brother repeats the displacement of destructive, anti-social tendencies shared by the protagonists onto a clearly defined upper-class scapegoat.

249–60 Leonato makes this clear in his hurried entrance with the Sexton, asking 'Which is the villain? Let me see his eyes' (V.i.249). He dismisses Borachio's confession that he 'alone' was responsible for killing Hero, looking past him to address the real villains Don Pedro and Claudio. Leonato's sarcasm, like that of Antony in *Julius Caesar*, cuts to the truth in exposing the conduct of this 'pair of honourable men' as far from being brave or worthy (V.i.255–60).

261–87 Both men are publicly shamed and might show this through stance and gesture. Both readily submit themselves to any punishment that Leonato wishes to impose, yet both refuse to acknowledge any other sin except that of 'mistaking' or misinterpreting. It is thus not clear how deeply they understand or feel any guilt beneath their flamboyant willingness to do any 'penance' (V.i.261–68). Don Pedro claims that Borachio's news runs 'like iron' through the blood and Claudio professes 'I have drunk poison whiles he uttered it' (V.i.235–36). These two lines offer only a very flimsy skeleton for an actor to build a convincing sense of remorse. If Claudio is to be at all sympathetic the actor must react silently as Borachio speaks, showing through facial and bodily expressions a growing sense of horror at what Claudio has done. The line 'the lady is dead' (V.i.232) is the cue for a heightened response such as covering his face or head with his hands, weeping, screwing up his eyes and face in pain. By the time Leonato proposes the mourning ceremony and the substitute wedding, Claudio should be crying and claims he is (V.i.283). The swiftness with which he accepts Leonato's plan can, however, give the impression of an extremely shallow performance of grief. The actor who wishes to play Claudio sympathetically has an uphill struggle to convince spectators that these are not crocodile tears.

288–93 Borachio's eagerness to excuse Margaret and deny her complicity in the plot is not very credible as evidence of a virtuous reformation on his part but is easier to explain in terms of his affection for her, which by this stage, may also be partly strategic. In some performances Margaret comes onstage here with other members of the household, behind Leonato and the Sexton, and a look can pass between her and Borachio before he speaks. If they have been partnered in the dance in Act II scene i, this serves to show some kind of bond between them as a basis for Margaret's willingness to go along with Borachio's bizarre wooing game. Her social self-consciousness, including a sense of ambition, goes some way to explain her willingness to step into her lady's shoes, or fine clothes. The elevated window setting would make it clear to many early modern spectators that

Margaret is not pretending to be Leonato's Hero but rather Hero of Sestos, the heroine of Greek romance who secretly met with her lover Leander and gave him entrance to the tower in which she had immured herself. Play acting as Hero of Sestos gives a logic to Margaret's willingness to be wooed 'by the name of Hero' as she 'leans me out of her mistress' chamber window, bids me a thousand times good night' as though she were bidding farewell to Leander (III.iii.140–1). Although socially transgressive, her behaviour is still relatively innocent. For Borachio, a relationship with Margaret may constitute his best chance of securing a future position once he has demonstrated his remorse and been duly punished.

294–315 Dogberry's farewell performance is a wonderful set piece that has the effect of shifting the mood for a happy ending. He is careful to remember the public matter of 'one Deformed' as well as the more personal offence in Conrade's ignominious defamation of him as 'an ass'. By bringing together the courtly figure of fashion who 'wears a key in his ear and a lock hanging by it' and the common officer who is an ass, Dogberry once again inadvertently warns the aristocratic assembly onstage about the dangers of their love of superficial display, self-absorption, folly and ignorance. 'I beseech your worship to correct yourself, for the example of others' (V.i.311–12) is not just a joke and should be delivered with the same earnest attention to duty and protocol that animates Dogberry throughout. His farewell, giving Leonato 'leave to depart' from his own house, is a suitable climax to Dogberry's minutely orchestrated deformation of ceremonial protocols, the comic equivalent of the broken nuptial. Since Dogberry has accidentally brought so many truths to light, his emphatic wish that God may prohibit the wished-for 'merry meeting' (V.i.314) may cast a shadow over the reunion of Claudio and Hero.

316–18 Shakespeare leaves Don Pedro and Claudio silent onstage for 31 lines during the exchange with Dogberry. Their non-verbal behaviour is a means to shape the audience's response. If they smile at Dogberry's performance, such willingness to turn their attention to lighter matters can easily mark their remorse, and Claudio's attachment to Hero, as superficial. If, however, they take a cue from Leonato's 'I take my leave' to turn away from the assembled company and continue to show shame, grief and remorse at the margins of the stage, Don Pedro's words 'We will not fail' and Claudio's 'Tonight I'll mourn with Hero' (V.i.318) garner more respect from those on and offstage.

319–20   Leonato's final reference to Borachio and Conrade cues their exits (led either by members of the Watch or by Leonato's servants) and Margaret's entrance.

Act V, scene ii

Leonato's final lines in the previous scene serve to introduce Margaret here. If she is not onstage in V.i a simultaneous exit and entrance and cross-over of performers gives an opportunity for a significant look or gesture to pass between Margaret and the 'bound' Borachio, or for her to pointedly ignore him while flirting with Benedick. This scene takes place outside, a suitable setting being the orchard in which the love plot was staged. Benedick follows Margaret, anxious to speak to Beatrice.

1–25   Margaret may be deliberately teasing him by asking him to write a sonnet in praise of her beauty, knowing from gossip with Hero and Beatrice that he 'cannot woo in festival terms' (V.ii.40). Alternatively, her attempts to attract his romantic attention may be half serious, part of her social aspirations to rise above stairs through marriage and become mistress of a household rather than a servant. Benedick is certainly a much better catch than Borachio, especially if she has just seen him on the way to prison. By running away from Benedick, Margaret can force him to make bodily contact in his attempt to catch her. Her suggestive innuendo in 'no man shall come over me' and in the discussion of weapons which follows, demonstrates that Leonato was quite wrong in attributing all lewdness to Borachio (V.i.320). Margaret's demand 'Give us the swords' (V.ii.19) makes her sound, superficially at least, like Beatrice. In Act III scene iv, Margaret competed with Beatrice in witty repartee and a production can usefully draw parallels between them in terms of Margaret copying Beatrice's style of coiffure, dress or mannerisms. To Margaret, however, swords are references to sex while to Beatrice they are weapons for killing. When Margaret says 'Give us the swords', a turn of the head by the Benedick actor can show that his mind moves to Beatrice so that the thought that they are 'dangerous weapons for maids' loses the buzz of innuendo. Margaret senses immediately that Benedick has lost interest in her and promises, perhaps a little sulkily, to call Beatrice.

25–40 Benedick looks around to check that Margaret is safely offstage before practising his song. He is sensible enough to know how bad a singer and poet he is, freely admitting this to the audience. He fills the following, agonising, wait for Beatrice with talk of true lovers, phrase after phrase tumbling over each other to show his nervousness. He may then resort to busying his fingers with a pencil and paper from his pocket as he confides his shortcomings as a poet.

41–84 Finally, to his relief, Beatrice enters. She jests but might show a slight reserve until she hears what she came for: 'what hath passed between you and Claudio' (V.ii.46). They can then relish the depth of mutual affection that now undergirds their battle of wit. Benedick's phrase 'thou and I are too wise to woo peaceably' (V.ii.67) might be infused with a delight in friendship as well as romance and sexual attraction. They are both animated in debate over self-adulation, so much so that, after Benedick has finished praising himself, Beatrice seems to be struck by a sense of guilt in her own happiness as the thought of her cousin's fate crosses her mind. Some facial expression prompts the sensitive Benedick to ask 'And now tell me, how doth your cousin? … And how do you?' (V.ii.81–83).

85–95 Ursula should run on (in spite of her age) with the news of latest developments inside the house. She might smile in delight to show her joy at the clearing of Hero's name and excitement as to what will happen next, emotions shared by Beatrice and Benedick. Beatrice's formal invitation 'Will you go hear this news, signor?' can be accompanied by a gesture inviting him into the house or offering Benedick her hand. His relief that the violence of the duel is now transmuted into a sexual death in Beatrice's lap marks his full transformation from soldier to lover, albeit in terms that mock the courtly convention. 'I will go with thee to thine uncle's' might be a cue to take her arm, and the two exit as a couple with Ursula running ahead.

Act V, scene iii

The mood, pace and lighting changes dramatically for this night-time scene of mourning which takes place at Leonato's monument. Although the scene has only 33 lines it should play longer, allowing plenty of time for pauses between the speeches and a slow procession around the tomb. Its ritual complexity, involving spectacle, coordinated movement, music, song, and the epitaph as material prop, needs to be fully articulated in the theatre if it is to achieve its effect as a counterpoint to the wedding ceremony of Act IV scene i. Since the audience have been previously complicit in Hero's fate, albeit by their silent witnessing of the desecrated wedding, this scene constitutes an important means to integrate them with the onstage action of repentance via the public performance of ritual.

The actors carry tapers, informing spectators that this is the dark night of the wedding, and of the soul for Claudio and Don Pedro. The actors are in mourning and should enter in an ordered procession led by Don Pedro and Claudio, who is holding the epitaph. Some kind of structure is required to represent Leonato's family monument: the tomb in which Hero is supposedly buried. A reconfiguration of the altar at which Claudio rejected her will evoke memories of the former scene. It may be decorated with the wedding flowers (following the directions given by Capulet in *Romeo and Juliet* IV.v.84–90) or material memorials such as Hero's gloves. Alternatively, if a statue of Cupid was used in the orchard scenes the Cupid could be replaced on the plinth by a sacrificial cross, a sleeping effigy of Hero (perhaps embodied by the same actor), a *memento mori* like a skull, or a reference to Diana, goddess of chastity to whom the song is addressed. Whatever the directorial choice, the effect should be to evoke a solemn, poignant sense of loss.

1–10 Claudio opens the proceedings by citing the reading of the epitaph precisely at 'the monument of Leonato', the location confirmed by 'A Lord'. The text of the epitaph is not clearly designated to a speaker since there is no further speech prefix for the lines following the word *Epitaph* printed in the quarto. It would seem logical for Claudio to speak the epitaph in accordance with his promise to Leonato (V.i.274–75), and, since this inscription is obviously a piece of detachable script, to be carried by the actor, this may explain why the speech prefix is missing. A public rehearsal of Claudio's guilt, an acknowledgement of his *slanderous tongue* and its mortifying effect, ritually transfers the shame from Hero to himself. If he directs these words at an effigy of Hero who is played by the Hero actor, then her body is literally cleared of slander and she can witness Claudio's penitence first hand. Claudio then symbolically places the object from which he read the text – an engraved plaque or a written scroll – onto the tomb as a lasting testimony of Hero's innocence and his own guilt. If, paying strict attention to the quarto's previous speech prefix, the epitaph is spoken and hung on the tomb by an anonymous Lord, its confessional power becomes communal rather than personal. The speaker's impersonal intonation speaks for everyone who shares in the shame of having contributed, however passively, to the destruction of the wedding and of Hero as bride. Offstage spectators can, arguably, access the penitential dimension of the ritual for themselves more easily via the anonymous voice. To compensate for any loss of sympathy caused by taking these lines away from Claudio, the actor could play as though too distressed to speak, a symptom easily recognisable by those who have experienced the funerals of loved ones.

11–23 Even if he does not speak much, Claudio is the internal director and protagonist of the scene. He cues the music and the singing of a 'solemn hymn' to Diana. The non-singers, including Claudio, participate kinaesthetically in the appeal for her forgiveness by going 'round about' Hero's tomb clockwise in orderly steps, to ward off evil spirits (V.iii.16). A silent Claudio may lead the procession, coming full circle with a promise to repeat 'this rite' annually (V.iii.23). The circular movement is an important revolution: a turning round which is also a coming back to the beginning so that a second wedding can follow to complete the play.

24–33 Don Pedro commands the mourners to 'put your torches out', signalling the shift from mourning to morning (V.iii.24). In a modern theatre, his reference to the grey light of dawn and the imminent arrival of the 'wheels of Phoebus' (V.iii.26), the sun, cues a gradual lighting change. This, in turn, prompts Don Pedro to direct a change to 'other weeds' or clothes for the wedding so that Claudio can look forward to the blessing of Hymen, god of marriage, whose traditional colour was yellow (V.ii.30–32).

Act V, scene iv

1–9 The opening of this scene picks up on the energy of the new day and is busy with a sense of righteous self-congratulation among the men, who gossip together about the outcome of events. They are a 'fair assembly' (V.iv.34), formally dressed and with new floral decorations. A production might stage silent exchanges between Hero, Ursula, Beatrice and Margaret as they arrange each other's attire, abuzz with anticipation about the postponed wedding. When Margaret is singled out for her 'fault' again, the female group can look up, forcing Leonato to qualify his remark with the words 'Although against her will' (V.iv.1–4). Benedick is now part of Leonato's male family group, as Beatrice can notice with pleasure in anticipation of his formal approach to her uncle.

10–33 Leonato stage manages the scene, first sending the ladies offstage to a private chamber in the house with the instruction that they be masked. A scrambled exit accompanied by excited giggles can create an atmosphere of anticipation. Antonio is then given directions. If, as would be natural, Leonato is again in a nervous state, Antonio's promise to perform his part 'with confirmed countenance' (V.iv.17) is made to reassure his brother, and might involve putting an affectionate arm around him. This leaves Benedick free to approach the Friar and then make a request for Leonato's permission to marry Beatrice. Benedick's uneasiness at entering such new territory will undoubtedly be increased by Leonato's 'enigmatical' references to the overhearing plots (V.iv.27). They serve as a useful distraction to calm the father's nerves even as they mystify Benedick. A nervous smile can show he is grateful to hear Leonato's blessing and a promise of help from the Friar, who moves into his position next to Antonio. Nevertheless, Benedick remains unprepared as the formal proceedings begin. Don Pedro comments, doubtless with deliberate exaggeration, on his 'February face / So full of frost, of storm and cloudiness' (V.iv.41–42).

34–51 The Prince and Count probably enter downstage of Leonato, who is curiously empowered by his ex-officio position, having relinquished the role of father-of-the-bride to his brother. Although he says to Claudio 'I do give you her' (V.iv.53), perhaps he no longer physically gives Hero away so the loss of his daughter to another man is now less traumatic. He cues Antonio to fetch the masked ladies with a confidence we have not seen before. To fill the awkward time waiting for the ladies to appear, Don Pedro and Claudio tease Benedick. He has had no opportunity to formally retract his challenge and might show by his expression that he finds their cuckoldry jokes in bad taste: partly because of his own imminent marriage but also because they indicate little sense of remorse on the part of the princes, and show a lack of respect for the solemnity of the occasion. Both these reasons motivate Benedick's cutting retort to Claudio about having the 'bleat' of an immature bastard (V.iv.48–51). The formal entrance of the masked group with Antonio prevents this hostility from escalating into violence, a violence which should now have been dispersed by the resolution of the plot.

Enter ANTONIO, HERO, BEATRICE, MARGARET *and* URSULA *[the women masked]*   The four female characters should, in theory, be indistinguishable because their faces are covered with either masks or veils. Leonato directs them to enter 'masked' but the quarto does not specify how; directorial choice helps to shape what kind of a ritual this scene stages. Masks recall the ball of Act II scene i, thus defining the joining of couples at the end of the play as a betrothal. Veiled figures invoke memories of the earlier wedding, especially if the female characters hold flowers. This sets the closing moments of the play back at the beginning of the postponed wedding, a reading supported by the Friar's invitation 'to the chapel let us presently', meaning immediately (V.iv.71). In spite of their face coverings, the actors' physical shapes (Beatrice being much taller than Hero) will make their identities fairly transparent to off and onstage spectators.

52–59   Claudio is, importantly, denied the right to see his fiancée's face until he has taken her hand and promised to marry her 'before this Friar'. He must compensate for his earlier blindness to her innocence by demonstrating absolute faith in his new bride without seeing her. How she responds to his invitation of 'give me your hand' – whether immediately or more slowly and perhaps with reluctance – can communicate to spectators how Hero now feels about Claudio. His gesture of taking her hand and the promise 'I am your husband if you like of me' (V.iv.59), witnessed by on and offstage audiences, finally effects the pledge he refused to give earlier in the church.

60–64 This is the cue for Hero to reveal her identity and reinvoke her earlier pledge. Tone will convey how Hero feels about this second wedding and her future with Claudio. Her lines are also a reaffirmation of self, which might be more important than a dedication of herself to him. She transcends her dishonoured identity: 'one Hero died defiled', and reasserts a resurrected self saying 'but I do live / And surely as I live, I am a maid' (V.iv.62–64).

65–66 Amidst the wonder of this apparent miracle, Don Pedro and Claudio's exclamations sound a rather more sinister note for the future. By repeating Hero's name 'Another Hero!' and 'The former Hero! Hero that is dead!' (V.iv.62 and 65), they recall the tragic heroine of Greek myth, the licentious woman who 'did talk with a man out at a window' (IV.i.307). Hero's overdetermined name and the legacy it brings means that she will always be open to suspicion, born out of male insecurity about female sexuality. She has no subject position other than that of 'the former Hero, Hero that is dead' and has no reply to Don Pedro's authoritative labelling of her. The root causes of the potential tragedy can thus still be glimpsed beneath the happiness of the reunion.

66–72 The Friar's haste to conclude his rescue plan with 'holy rites' and get everyone offstage to the chapel makes Benedick's intervention all the more noticeable and embarrassing (V.iv.69–72).

73–96 Beatrice and Benedick's quickfire equivocations suspend the moment of romantic fulfilment once again, tantalising the audience and the characters. A stand-off occurs because of the highly public nature of the scene in which the pride of both is at stake (V.iv.74–83). Neither is willing to move, as the blocking of the scene with an apparently unbridgeable distance between them should indicate. Once again, they must rely on their friends' intervention to bring them together using the evidence of their love sonnets to each other, more notes worth the noting. In this sense, the exchange offers a comic reprise of the overhearing scenes, a comic 'miracle' to parallel the more serious resurrection of Hero and Claudio's wedding.

97   In the quarto, it is the stage manager Leonato who comes forward to command peace from the couple who are too wise to woo peaceably. His authoritative direction to Beatrice – 'I will stop your mouth' (V.iv.97) – is a somewhat surprising assertion of patriarchal authority but entirely in keeping with his status as Beatrice's guardian. Since he could not give his daughter away, formally handing over his niece to Benedick is a belated though satisfying, and perhaps more comfortable, alternative. In spite of its appearance of heavy-handed paternal direction, this is a more egalitarian resolution than that suggested by editions and productions which give the lines to Benedick. If Benedick takes Beatrice's hand, commands and stops her mouth with a kiss, the play concludes with a rather uncomfortable taming of Beatrice's wild heart to his loving hand (III.i.112). One senses that the actor has more to say in defence of that assertive, independent Beatrice. Spoken softly and lovingly, however, Benedick could give the line a powerfully erotic charge. A way of realising both romantic and formal closure would be for Leonato to speak the line and hand Beatrice to Benedick, who then kiss, stopping each other's mouths.

98–117   By this point Ursula and Margaret will also have unmasked, the former might join Leonato and Antonio and look fondly on the happiness of the younger-generation couples, while the forgiven Margaret may be reunited with Borachio for the final dance or may be unpartnered. Don Pedro's isolation among the younger generation is suggested by his teasing of Benedick, which provokes Benedick's defence of himself and marriage. Non-verbal gestures of some kind may be used by signal the reconciliation between Claudio and Benedick before the couples take hands in anticipation of a dance.

120–26   Benedick's comment 'Prince, thou art sad – get thee a wife, get thee a wife' (V.iv.120) after he has announced the dance probably signals Don Pedro's isolation. If Don Pedro moves forward to dance with Margaret, this produces an unexpectedly exciting ending for the socially ambitious servant. If Margaret is paired with Borachio, Antonio or Leonato for the dance, Don Pedro is left alone. His soldier companions have disappeared and in a modern production lighting effects can point up his sense of loneliness. The announcement of his brother's return to Messina in the closing lines sets up the possibility of an uneasy pairing based on sameness and opposition, perhaps symbolising internal divisions and self-loathing that Don Pedro is left to confront in the midst of what appears to be a cohesive society based on marriage. There is no stage direction for Don John to be brought back onstage, but this is a possibility in production. Benedick's dismissal of anything that can be said against marriage has verbally closed the circle of heterosexual coupling. His call to 'strike up pipers' (V.iv.126) cues musicians and the beginning of a dance to which all are invited but in which not all can participate.

3   Intellectual and Cultural
Contexts

Timbreo and Fenicia, Novella XXII *La Prima Parte de le Novelle de Bandello*

The setting and the character names of *Much Ado* are derived from one of Matteo Bandello's stories in *La Prima Parte de le Novelle*, published in Italian in 1554 and translated into French by Belleforrest in *Histoire Tragiques* (1569). Many of the plot details in Bandello parallel those in *Much Ado*, while the divergences suggest a desire for different dramatic effects.

King Piero of Arragon and his French forces return to Messina having put down a Sicilian rebellion. At the extensive victory celebrations with 'joustings and balls being held daily', one of his courtiers, Sir Timbreo de Cardona, falls in love with Fenicia, daughter of Messer Lionato de' Lionati. Fenicia modestly refuses his advances, affirming 'that she intended to keep her maidenhood inviolate for the man who would be given her as a husband' (Bullough, 1958, 113). He asks for her hand in marriage, assured that she 'came of ancient and noble stock' even though she is not a member of the royal Court. Fenicia thanks God 'who had granted so glorious an outcome of her chaste love; and her face showed that she was glad'. However, a rival for her love, the well-reputed courtier and soldier Sir Girondo Olerio Valenziano, is driven by his passionate 'frenzy of amorous desire' into a plot to destroy the match: 'blameworthy in anyone, let alone a knight and gentleman' (Bullough, 1958, 114).

In Bandello's story, Sir Girondo suborns a 'fellow of little upbringing, more pleased with evil than with good' to inform Timbreo that he knows a friend who makes love to Fenicia often two or three times a week. Girondo duly sets up his 'perfumed' henchman to bring a ladder and climb up to the window of 'an ancient salon', which Fenicia occasionally uses to look out over the garden of Master Lionato's house (Bullough, 1958, 115–16). Sir Girondo is concealed in a ruined house opposite to watch. The henchman plays his part well, pointing out the need for quiet (loudly enough for Girondo to hear) because 'my lady Fenicia told me that you had leaned it [the ladder] there with too much noise' (Bullough, 1958, 117). Although Sir Timbreo does not see a lady at the window at all, his feelings transform dramatically:

> [B]eing convinced that the man who had climbed up had gone in to lie with Fenicia, he felt himself swooning, overborne with the keenest suffering. But so powerfully did his righteous anger (as he thought it) work in him that it banished every feeling of jealousy, and not only froze the sincere and burning love which he bore for Fenicia, but converted it into cruel hate.
>
> (Bullough, 1958, 117)

Sir Timbreo does not shame Fenicia in the church but sends a message that is read out in front of the whole family. While Messer Lionato thinks Sir Timbreo's change is for reasons of social status and snobbery rather than giving any credit to the story of Fenicia's licentiousness, Fenicia herself is struck to the quick.

> Hearing this bitter and contemptuous message Fenicia stood as though stricken dead, as did her father and mother. But regaining life and breath (which had almost failed in his amazement), Messer Lionato said to the messenger, 'Friend, I always feared, from the first moment when you spoke to me of this marriage, that Sir Timbreo would not stand firm to his request, for I knew then as I do now that I am only a poor gentleman and not his equal. Yet surely if he repented of his promise to make her his wife it would have been sufficient for him to declare that he did not want her, and not to have laid against her this injurious accusation of whoredom. It is indeed true that all things are possible, but I know how my daughter has been reared and what her habits are. God, who is our just Judge will one day, I believe, make known the truth'.
>
> (Bullough, 1958, 118)

Fenicia sinks into grief and despair at hearing herself accused so wrongly, and loses the will to live; so that, struck down with deep sorrow, she sank down 'like a dead woman, and suddenly losing her native hues she looked more like a marble statue rather than a living creature' (Bullough, 1958, 119). She is taken to bed and revived with hot cloths. Doctors are summoned and it is rumoured through Messina that she was close to death.

The most dramatic element of the Bandello story is the supposed death and revival of Fenicia, which may well have provided the inspiration for scenes of female resurrection in Shakespeare's romances: the revival of Thaisa in *Pericles* and of Hermione in *The Winter's Tale* (see Mueller, 1994). A strong matriarchal presence guides the plot in Bandello's text, from the point when female relatives and friends come to comfort Fenicia and blame Sir Timbreo with bitter words. Shakespeare, of course, cuts Hero's mother out of the spoken script altogether and gives Beatrice only limited effectiveness in resolving the situation, reserving the powerful matriarchs for his late plays. In Bandello, Fenicia asks for her female relatives' silence and gives what appears to be a deathbed speech protesting her innocence and claiming it is the slander to her honour rather than the fact of being rejected that has cut her heart strings.

> I know that I shall be eternally blamed by all in Messina for a sin which I not only never committed but indeed never thought of committing. Nevertheless, like a common strumpet, I shall always be pointed at with the finger of scorn … May my father and mother and all our friends and relations have at least this small consolation in their trouble, that I am entirely innocent of the sin which has been laid against me, and may they take as witness my love which I give them, as an obedient daughter must do, since at present I can give them no greater pledge or testimony. It is enough for me that before the just tribunal of Christ I shall be known innocent of such baseness; and thus to Him who gave it I commend my soul, which longs to escape from this earthly prison and now takes its way toward Him.
>
> (Bullough, 1958, 119–20)

Fenicia then loses her speech, goes into a cold sweat, and appears to surrender herself to death. Household mourning is begun with all the 'spectators' drawn into the 'lamentable moan' (perhaps a detail that guided Shakespeare's designs to integrate spectators into the tragicomic Hero–Claudio plot). When Fenicia's mother and aunt begin to wash her body with warm water, however, Fenicia revives: her limbs warm and her heart flutters. She protests that it were better if she were dead, but her mother and aunt assure her that 'you must live, since God wills it and He will set things right' (Bullough, 1958, 121). Her mother and father, overjoyed at her recovery, secretly convey her to her uncle's house, a country villa, along with one of her sisters so that she can assume another identity and eventually be matched again. In public, the family go into ostentatious mourning, following the coffin that Fenicia's mother secretly filled and sealed with pitch. Her father inscribes an epitaph for Fenicia in which she declares herself 'still a virgin innocent of blame' who chose to die rather than be the object of finger-pointing scandals as a 'woman of ill-fame' (Bullough, 1958, 122).

Sir Girondo is overcome with guilt. He takes Timbreo into the chapel with the tomb, bares his breast, draws his sword and, having confessed his plotting, asks Timbreo to kill him as a just revenge. Timbreo's reaction speaks more strongly of male friendship than romantic love. He first promises 'I do not mean to take any revenge on you; for losing one friend after another would be to add grief to grief', and points out, logically, that nothing will bring Fenicia back from the dead. He only reproves Sir Girondo for one thing: not revealing his love for Fenicia; 'For then I should have relinquished my amorous enterprise to you before asking her father for her hand', he protests, and 'in overcoming myself I should have preferred our friendship to my desire' (Bullough, 1958, 125). These feelings prefigure the depiction of very strong bonds between the soldiers in *Much Ado*, especially between Don Pedro and Claudio. In Bandello's story, brotherly bonding strengthens when Girondo and Timbreo pray and weep at the tomb together, go and confess to Lionato and are both taken to the uncle's country villa for the final revelation scene. Timbreo has promised to take a wife of Lionato's choosing (paralleling Leontes's situation in *The Winter's Tale*) and Fenicia, renamed Lucilla, is presented to him without any veil or disguise. He does not recognise her but agrees to marry her immediately and, once the ceremony and wedding feast are begun, it is the aunt who refers back to Fenicia, causes Timbreo and Girondo to weep again, and Timbreo to declare that his love for Fenicia would last forever. Lionato comically reprimands him 'you demonstrate but poorly in deeds what you protest in your words', pointing out that 'having been married to your dearly beloved Fenicia and having sat all morning beside her, you still do not recognize her'. Timbreo does, finally recognise her and 'weeping for joy' they are reunited (Bullough, 1958, 130). Fenicia's appearance as a bride is described in the same kind of sensual detail as that found in Claudio's speeches about Hero 'as chaste as is the bud ere it be blown' (IV.i.57) in the wedding scene of *Much Ado*. Unlike the bitter and disillusioned Claudio, however, Bandello's narrator reads the bride's blush correctly:

> He who gazed on the charming colour of her face saw a gentle and pure whiteness tinged with a becoming and virginal blush, which not art but Mistress Nature painted with crimson now more, now less, according to her changing emotions and actions. Her swelling breast appeared like a graceful, living mass of gleaming alabaster, with a rounded throat that seemed like snow.
>
> (Bullough, 1958, 131)

Bandello's tale, like *Much Ado*, concludes with a double wedding celebration since Girondo requests the hand of her younger sister Belfiore. The villain's 'transformation' and reward thus makes for a more secure happy ending than the arrest of Don John alongside the marriage of Benedick to Beatrice in Shakespeare's text. The couples are received and fêted by King Piero and his queen, given court positions and royal dowries. This constitutes a much more lavish (unstageable) and firmly heterosexual conclusion than that presented in *Much Ado* by Benedick's throw-away comment to Don Pedro 'Prince, thou art sad – get thee a wife, get thee a wife' (V.ii.120).

Ariosto, *Orlando Furioso* (1591)

The Hero–Claudio plot is based on common folk motifs of disguise, love trysts at windows, and maids dressing as their mistresses. Versions of the window scene plot appear in Book II Canto IV of Spenser's *Faerie Queene* and in Munday's 1585 play *Fedele and Fortunio*, which may well have been recalled by early spectators of *Much Ado*. The fullest version immediately available to Shakespeare would have been Book V of Ariosto's *Orlando Furioso*, translated in 1591 by Sir John Harington. Two more Ariosto tales of jealousy and mistrust were translated by R.T. and published in 1597. In a fashion typical of folk ballad tradition Ariosto's Book V story is told in the first person, by Dalinda, the waiting gentlewoman who provides a very full and rich source for Shakespeare's slighter characterisation of Margaret.

She sets out the moral of her story in terms that resonate through the Hero–Claudio plot:

> Men seeke we see, and haue in euerie age,
> To foile their foes, and tread them in the dust.
> But there to wreake their rancour and their rage,
> Where they are lou'd, is foule and too vnjust.
> Loue should prevaile, just anger to asswage,
> If loue bring death, whereto can women trust?
> Yet loue did breede my daunger and my feare,
> As you shall heare if you will giue me eare.

Dalinda describes how she entered the service of Genevra, the Scottish princess, and fell in love with Polynesso, Duke of Albany, who was himself in love with Genevra, partly out of ambition to attain her hand in marriage. He persuaded Dalinda to play courtship games with him at Genevra's window, to court Genevra for him, and, eventually, to dress in her clothes:

> For entring first into my tender spring,
> Of youthfull yeares, vnto the court I came,
> And serued there the daughter of our king,
> And kept a place of honor with good fame,
> Till loue (alas that loue such care should bring)
> Enuide my state, and sought to do me shame.
> Loue made the Duke of Alban seeme to me,
> The fairest wight that erst mine eye did see … .
>
> (32)

> And (for I thought he lou'd me all aboue)
> I bent my selfe to hold and loue him best,
> But now I find that hard it is to proue,
> By sight or speech what bides in secret brest,
> While I (poore I) did thus beleeue and loue,
> He gets my bodie bed and all the rest.
> Nor thinking this might breed my mistres danger,
> I vsd this practise in *Geneuras* chamber.
>
> Where all the things of greatest value lay,
> And where *Geneura* sleepes her selfe sometime,
> There at a window we did finde away,

Secret and sure to couer this our crime:
Here when my loue and I were bent to play,
I taught him by a scale of cord to clime,
And at the window I my selfe would stand,
And let the ladder downe into his hand. . .

Not all of loue, but partly of ambition,
He beares in hand his minde is onely bent,
Because of her great state and hie condition,
To haue her for his wife is his entent:
He nothing doubteth of the kings permission,
Had he obtain *Geneuras* free assent.
Ne was it hard for him to take in hand,
That was the second person in the land. . .

(33)

Dalinda recounts how, although she attempted to further the Duke of Alban's suit, Genevra was in love with Ariodant, a knight from Italy who came to court with his brother (a pairing found again in Shakespeare in Claudio–Benedick and Don Pedro–Don John).

From Italy for seruice (as I heare)
Vnto the court he and his brother came,
In tourneys and in tilt he had no peere,
All Britain soone was filled with his fame.
Our king did loue him well and hold him deere,
And did by princely gifts confirme the same.
Castels and townes, and lordships, he him gaue,
And made him great, such power great princes haue.

Our soueraigne much, his daughter lykte him more,
And *Ariodant* this worthy knight is named,
So braue in deeds of armes himselfe he bore,
No Ladie of his loue need be ashamed:
The hill of Sicil burneth not so sore,
Nor is the mount Vesuuio so inflamed,
As *Ariodantes* heart was set on fire,
Geneuras beautie kindling his desire.

(33)

Genevra returns Ariodant's love and so rejects all Dalinda's attempts to promote the Duke Polynesso who is 'Greeu'd with repulse'. Once

Duke Polynesso's passionate love for Genevra cools and turns to hate, he determines to part Genevra and Ariodant 'by some vile and subtil traine' and to use Dalinda to his own devious ends. He explains his window plot in romantic terms:

Nor do I deeme so deare the great delight,
As I disdain I should be so reiect,
And lest this griefe should ouercome me quight,
Because I faile to bring it to effect,
To please my fond conceipt this very night,
Pray thee deare to do as I direct:
When faire *Geneura* to her bed is gone,
Take thou the clothes she ware and put them on.

As she is wont her golden haire to dresse,
In stately sort to wynd it on her wyre,
So you her person liuely to expresse,
May dresse your owne and weare her head attire,
Her gorgets and her iewels rich no lesse,
You may put on t'accomplish my desire,
And when vnto the window I ascend,
I will my comming there you do attend.

Thus I may passe my fancies foolish fit,
And thus (quoth he) my selfe I would deceave.
And I that had no reason, nor no wit,
His shamefull drift (though open) to perceave:
Wearinge my Mistresse robes that seru'd me fit,
And stood at window, there him to receave.
And of the fraud I was no whit aware,
Till that fell out that caused all my care.

(34)

Ariodant was friendly towards his rival, Duke Polynesso, but the latter taunted Ariodant with the proposal of a love contest between them in which they would share all their secrets. Ariodant first reveals the secret betrothal he has made with Genevra:

And first the stranger doth his state reueale,
Telling the truth in hope to end the strife,
How she had promisd him in wo and weale,
To liue with him, and loue him all her life.

And how with writing with her hand and seale,
She had confirmed she would be his wife,
Except she were forbidden by her father,
For then to liue vnmarride she had rather.

(34)

In response, Duke Polynesso sows seeds of jealousy and doubt in
Ariodant's mind:

Alas (quoth he) I see you do not know,
How cunningly these women can dissemble,
Litle to loue where they make greatest show,
And not to be the thing they most resemble,
But other fauours I receaue I trow,
When as we two do secretly assemble,
As I will tell you (though I should conceale it)
Because you promise neuer to reueale it.

The truth is this that I full oft haue seene
Her yvory corps, and bene with her all night,
And naked layne her naked armes betweene,
And full enioyne the frutes of loues delight:
Now iudge who hath in greatest fauour beene,
To which of vs she doth pertayne in right,
And then geve place, and yeeld to me mine owne,
Sith by iust proofes I now haue made it knowne.

(35)

Although Ariodant does not believe such 'shamefull lies', he challenges
Polynesso to provide him with ocular proof of Genevra's unfaithful
love. Polynesso conceals Ariodant in some ruined houses opposite
the window and calls on Dalinda to play her accustomed role as her
mistress. Ariodant, afraid of being attacked in the ruined house, asks
his brother to act as a look out

His brother would not his request denie,
And so went *Ariodant* into his place,
And vndiscouerd closely there did lie,
Till hauing looked there a little space,
The craftie Duke to come he might descrie,
That meant the chast *Geneura* to deface,
Who hauing made to me his wonted signes,
I let him downe the ladder made of lines.

The gowne I ware was white, and richly set,
With aglets, pearle, and lace of gold wel garnished,
My stately tresses couerd with a net
Of beaten gold most pure and brightly varnished.
Not thus content, the vaile aloft I let,
Which only Princes weare: thus stately harnished,
And vnder *Cupids* banner bent to fight,
All vnawares I stood in all their sight.

For why *Lurcanio* either taking care,
Lest *Ariodant* should in some danger go,
Or that he sought (as all desirous are)
The counsels of his dearest frend to know,
Close out of sight by secret steps and ware,
Hard at his heeles his brother followd so,
Till he was nearer come by fiftie paces,
And there againe him selfe he newly places.

But I that thought no ill securely came
Vnto the open window as I sayd,
For once or twice before I did the same,
And had no hurt, which made me lesse afrayd:
I can not bost (except I bost of shame)
When in her robes I had my selfe arayd,
Me thought before I was not much vnlike her,
But certaine now I seemed very like her.

(35)

Unsurprisingly, Ariodant sinks into grief and sorrow, makes a first attempt to kill himself with his sword, but is saved by his brother, who recommends he takes revenge instead:

You rather should some iust reuenge deuise,
As she deserues to bring her to confusion.
Sith we haue plainly seene with both our eyes,
Her filthie fact appeare without collusion.
Loue those that loue againe if you be wise,
For of my counsell this is the conclusion,
Put vp your sword against your selfe prepared,
And let her sinne be to the king declared.

(36)

Ariodant retreats from the Court and Genevra is brought news that he has thrown himself into the sea in despair. His brother, Lurcanio, explains the reason – Genevra's unchaste assignation – and says he will defend his accusation by combat. Although the Scottish King thinks the story must be false (a contrast to Leonato's ready belief in *Much Ado*), he condemns Genevra to death, according to Scottish law, unless a champion will fight successfully in single combat, to prove the accusation a lie.

> The King (of crime that thinkes *Geneura* cleare)
> Offers to marrie her to anie knight,
> That will in armes defend his daughter deare,
> And proue her innocent in open fight.
> Yet for all this no champion doth appeare,
> Such feare they haue of this *Lurcanios* might.
> One gazeth on another as they stand,
> But none of them the combat takes in hand ....

> The King that meanes to make a certaine triall,
> If faire *Geneura* guiltie be or no,
> (For still she stiffly stood in the deniall,
> Of this that wrought her vndeserued wo)
> Examines all her maids, but they reply all,
> That of the matter nothing they did know.
> Which made me seeke for to preuent the danger,
> The Duke and I might haue about the stranger.
>
> (37)

Out of love for Duke Polynesso, Dalinda warns him about the danger of their assignation becoming public and he promises to hide her away in his castle, but really plots to have her murdered. She reveals the truth to Renaldo (a dramatic basis for Benedick's intervention and challenge). Renaldo takes her to an inn in St Andrews and comes to declare the truth and fight to defend Genevra's honour, only to find a stranger knight has already taken up the challenge.

> Vnto S. Andrews towne he maketh hast,
> Whereas the King was set with all his trayne,
> Carefully wayting for the trumpets blast,
> That must pronounce his daughters ioy or payne,
> But now *Renaldo* spurred had so fast,
> He was arriu'd within a mile or twayne,
> Through the village as he then was ryding,
> He met a page that brought them fresher tyding.

How there was come a warriour all disguised,
That meant to proue *Lurcanio* said vntrew,
His colours and his armour well deuised,
In manner and in making very new:
Sondry thereof in sundry wise surmised,
But who it was for certaine no man knew:
His page demaunded of his masters name,
Did sweare he neuer heard it since he came ...

(37)

Straight was it told him by the standers by,
How there was thither come a stranger knight,
That meant *Geneuras* innocence to trye,
And that already was begun the fight:
How that faire greene that next the wall did lye,
Was rayld about of purpose for the sight.
This newes did make *Renaldo* hasten in,
And leaue behind *Dalinda* at her Inne.

(38)

Renaldo's intervention to accuse Duke Polynesso prevents the fight between Lurcanio and the stranger knight, and a combat in which Renaldo defeats the Duke ensues:

Renaldos person with the tale he told,
Mou'd so the king, that straight without delay,
The knights were bidden both their hands to hold,
The combat for a time was causd to stay,
Then he againe with voyce and courage bold,
The secret of the matter doth bewray;
Declaring plaine how *Polynessos* lecherie
Had first contriu'd and now betrayd his trecherie.

Proffring of this to make a perfect proofe,
By combat hand to hand with sword and speare:
The Duke was cald that stood not farre aloofe,
And scantly able to conceale his feare;
First he denies, as was for his behoofe,
And straight to battell both agreed were,
Armd they were both, the place before was readie,
Now must they fight there could be no remedie.

How was the king, how were the people glad,
That faire *Geneura* faultlesse there did stand,

As Gods great goodnesse now reuealed had,
And should be proued by *Renaldos* hand.
All thought the Duke of mind and manners bad,
The proudst and cruelst man in all the land,
Likely it was as euery one surmised,
That this deceipt by him should be deuised.

Now *Polynesso* stands with doubtfull brest,
With fainting heart, with pale dismayed face,
Their trumpets blue, they set their spears in rest,
Renaldo commeth on a mightie pace,
For at this fight he finish will the feast,
And where to strike him he designs a place:
His verie first encounter was so fierce,
Renaldos speare the t'others sides did pierce.

And hauing ouerthrowne the Duke by force,
As one vnable so great strokes to bide,
And cast him cleane sixe paces from his horse,
Himselfe allights and th'others helme vntide,
Who making no resistance like a corse,
With faint low voyce for mercie now he cride,
And plaine confest with this his latter breath,
The fault that brought him this deserued death.

No sooner had he made this last confession,
But that his life did faile him with his voyce.
Geneuras double scape of foule oppression,
In life and fame did make the King reioyce:
Rather then her to leese his crownes possession,
He would haue wisht, if such had bene his choice:
To leese his realme he could haue bene no sadder:
To get it lost he could haue bene no gladder.

(38)

The stranger knight watches these developments from the sidelines
and the book ends with a cliffhanger, with 'who it was' to be revealed
'in another booke'. Book 6 reveals that the stranger is, of course, Ariodant,
and casts some interesting light on the formation of Claudio's character.
It begins by moralising Polynesso's tale in general terms that, by impli-
cation, also apply to Ariodant's doubt and despair:

Wretched is he, that thinks by doing ill,
His euill deedes long to conceale and hide,

For though the voice and toungs of men be still,
By foules or beasts his sin shalbe discride:
And God oft worketh by his secret will,
That sinne it selfe the sinner so doth guide,
That of his owne accord, without request,
He makes his wicked doings manifest. . . .

He whom *Geneura* wofully did waile,
He whom *Lurcanio* deemed to be dead,
He whom the king and court did so bewaile,
He that to all the realme such care had bred,
Doth liue; the clownes report in this did faile,
On which false ground the rumor false was spred.
And yet in this the peasant did not mocke,
He saw him leape downe headlong from the rock.

But as we see men oft with rash entent
Are desperate and do resolue to die,
And straight do change that fancy and repent,
When vnto death they do approch more nie:
So *Ariodant* to drowne himselfe that ment,
Plung'd in sea repented by and by,
And being of his limbes able and strong,
Vnto the shore he swam againe erre long.

And much dispraised in his inward thought,
This fond conceit that late his minde possest,
At last a blinde and narrow path him brought,
Weerie and wet to be an hermits guest:
With whom to stay in secret sort he sought,
Both that he might his former griefe digest,
And learne the truth, whether the clownes report,
Were by *Geneura* tane in griefe or sport.

(41)

News of Genevra's grief convinces Ariodant that she does love him and he resolves to defend her honour in combat, even though this is against his own brother, partly because he believes she may be innocent and, more fundamentally, because he wants to save her life, feeling that he will have no life without her. Finally, by defending her he will also prove that his love for her is greater than Polynesso's.

Alas (quoth he) I neuer shall abide,
Her through my cause to die in wo and paine,

Danger or death what ever do betide,
After her death my life cannot remaine,
She is my saint, in her my blisse doth bide,
Her golden rayes my eyes light still maintaine,
Fall backe, fall edge, and be it wrong or right,
In her defence I am resolu'd to fight.

I take the wrong, but yet Ile take the wrong
And die I shall, yet if I die I care not,
But then alas, by law she dies er long,
O cruell lawes so sweete a wight that spare not:
Yet this small ioy I finde these griefes among,
That *Polinesso* to defend her dare not,
And she shall finde how little she was loued,
Of him that to defend her neuer moued …

And thus resolued, he gets him armour new,
New horse and all things new that needfull beene
Clad all in blacke, a sad and mournfull hew,
Crost with a wreath of yellow and of greene,
A stranger bare his sheeld that neither knew,
His masters name nor him before had seene,
And thus as I before reherst, disguised
He met his brother as he had deuised.

(42)

It is by these means that Ariodant shows himself 'a truer lover' and so redeems himself 'that after so great wrong, entended / Against his brother her to haue defended'. He is rewarded with the gift of '*Geneura* bright' and Polynesso's dukedom which reverts to the crown and is given as her dowry. Dalinda receives a royal pardon and vows 'with honest mind & staid, / To liue her life in prayre and penitent', retiring to a nunnery (42).

The *querelle des femmes*

English examples of this literary debate between the sexes, fashionable in Europe right the way through the 15th, 16th and 17th centuries, are an important cultural context for *Much Ado*, particularly the battle of wits between Benedick and Beatrice. On the one hand, women's vices were listed as evidence against marriage and, on the other, defences of women listed their virtues. The following extracts from John Lyly's *The Anatomy of Wit* (1578) and *Jane Anger, Her Protection for Women*

(1589) offer a sample of advice to men and women to avoid loving the opposite sex, the tradition on which Beatrice and Benedick's 'merry war' draws.

The Anatomy of Wit (1578)

Lyly's text recounts the story of how Euphues and his younger friend Philautus were both rejected by Lucilla, an Italian gentlewoman. She objects to a match with Philautus arranged 'before I know the Bridegroome', protests 'the sweetness that I have found in the undefiled estate of virginity, causeth me to loathe the sour sauce which is mixed with matrimony' (26), and then declares her love for a simpleton, Curio, instead. Euphues pronounces an angry valediction: 'farewell *Lucilla*, the most inconstant that ever was nursed in *Naples*, farewell *Naples* the most cursed town in all Italy, and women all farewell' and continues with a diatribe against women: 'O the counterfaite love of women. Oh inconstant sex' (34v). His sense of injury gives rise to a misogynist diatribe typical of the *querelle* genre, entitled 'A cooling card for Philautus and all fond lovers'. His lamentations about wasting his time 'wholly to the service of women' and his advice to lovers to conceal and smother their passion rather than reveal it, offer a template for many of Benedick's views in *Much Ado*.

> [T]o spende my lyfe in the lappes of Ladyes, my lands in maintenance of brauery, my wit in the vanities of idle Sonnets. I had thought women had been as we men, that is true, faithful, zealous, constant, but I perceive they be rather woe unto men, by their falsehood, jealousy, inconstancy.
>
> (35r)

> Laye before thine eyes the slights and deceits of thy Lady, hir snatching in jest, and keeping in earnest, hir perjurie, her impietie, the countenaunce she sheweth to thee of course, the love she beareth to others of zeale, her open malice, her dissembled mischief.
>
> O I would in repeating their vices thou couldest be as eloquent, as in remembring them thou oughtest to be penitent: be she never so comely call her counterfaite, be she never so strayght think her crooked. And wreste all partes of hir bodye to the worst be she never so worthye. If she be well sette, then call hir a Bosse [i.e. fat], if slender, a Hasill twigge, if Nutbrowne, as blacke as a coale, if well coloured, a paynted wall, if she be pleasaunt, then is she a wanton, if sullenne, a clowne, if honeste, then is she coye [reclusive], if impudent, a harlotte.

Searche euery vayne and sinew of their disposition, if she haue no sighte in deskante, desire her to chaunt it, if no cunning to daunce request her to trippe it, if no skill in Musicke, proffer hir the Lute, if an ill gate, then walke with hir, if rude in speech, talke with hir, if she be gaggetoothed, tell her some merry jeste to make hir laughe, if pinke-eyed, some dolefull Historye, to cause her weepe, in the one her grinning will shewe her deformed, in the other her whininge, like a Pigge halferosted.

It is a worlde to see how commonly we are blynded, with the collusions of woemen and more enticed by their ornaments being artificiall, then their proportion being naturall. I loathe almost to thincke on their oyntments, and Apothecarie drugges [cosmetics], the sleeking of their faces, and all their slibber sawces, which bring quasiness to the stomacke, and disquyet to the minde.

Take from them, their periwiggs, their payntings, their Jewells, their rowles, their boulsterings, and thou shalt soone perceive that a woman is the least parte of her selfe. When they be once robbed of their robes, then will they appeare so odious, so ugly, so monstrous, that thou wilt rather thinke them Serpents than Saynts, & so lyke Hags, that thou wilt feare rather to be enchaunted then enamoured …

Moreouer to make thee the more stronger, to strive against these *Syrenes*, and more subtill to deceive these tame Serpentes, my counsel is that thou haue more strings to thy bow then one … the minde enamoured on two women, is lesse affected with desire, and lesse infected with despaire, one love expelleth an other, and the remembraunce of the latter quencheth the concupiscence of the first.

Yet if thou bee so weake being bewitched with their wiles that thou hast neither will to eschue, nor wit to avoyd their company … or so wedded that thou canst not abstaine from their glaunces, yet at the leaste dissemble thy griefe: If thou be as hot as the mount *Aetna*, faine thy self as cool as the hil *Caucasus*, carry two faces in one hood, couer thy flaming fancie with fained ashes, shew thy selfe sounde when thou art rotten, lette thy hew be merrye, when thy heart is melancholy: … thus dissembling thy griefe, thou mayest recure thy disease. Loue creepeth in by stealth and by stealth slideth away.

(43v–44v)

Jane Anger, Her Protection for Women. To defend them against the Scandalous Reportes of a late Surfeting Lover (1589)

This is a reply to a recently published attack on women (now lost, but possibly based on Lyly's text). It complains about 'the innumerable number of bookes to that purpose' published 'of late' (B1v) and sets out to contradict their misogyny, while warning women about the dangers of falling in love. Although Jane Anger's name is probably a pseudonym, a strong proto-feminist voice, not unlike that of Beatrice, emerges in the text:

> To all Women in generall and gentle Reader whatsoever.
>
> Fie on the falshoode of men, whose minds goe oft a madding, & whose tongues can not so soone be wagging, but straight they fal a railing. Was there ever any so abused, so slaundered, so railed upon, or so wickedly handeled vndeservedly, as are we women? Will the Gods permit it, the Goddesses stay their punishing judgments, and we ourselves not pursue their undoinges for such divelish practises. O Paules steeple and Charing Crosse! A halter hold al such persons. Let the streames of the channels in London streates run so swiftly, as they may be able to carry them from that saunctuarie. Let the stones be as Ice, the soales of their shooes as Glasse, the ways steep like Aetna, & every blast a Whyrl-wind puffed out of Boreas his long throat, that these may hasten their passage to the Devil's haven. Shall Surfeiters raile on our kindness, you stand still & say nought, and shall not Anger stretch the vaines of her brains, the stringes of her fingers, and the listes of her modestie, to answere their Surfeitings? Yes, truely. And herein I conjure all you to aide and assist me in defence of my Willingnes, which shall make me rest at your commandes. Fare you well.
>
>   Your friend. Ja. A. (A4v)
>
> The greatest fault that doth remain in us women is, that we are too credulous, for could we flatter as they can dissemble, and use our wittes well, as they can their tongues ill, then never would any of them complain of surfeiting. (B2v)
>
> Our good toward them is the destruction of our selves, we being wel formed, are by them fouly deformed: of our true meaning they make mockes, rewarding our loving follies with disdainful floutes: we are the griefe of men, in that wee take the griefe from man: we languish when they laugh, we lie sighing when they sit singing, and sit sobbing when they lie slugging and sleeping. (B3)
>
> We are contrary to men, because they are contrarie to that which is good: because they are spur blind, they cannot see into our natures, and we too well (though we had but half an eie) into their conditions, because they are so bad: our behaviours alter daily because men's virtues decay hourly. If Hesiodus had with equity as well looked into the life of man, as he did precisely search out the qualities of us women, he would have said, that if a woman trust unto a man, it shall fare as well with her,

as if she had a waight of a thousand pounds tied about her neck, and then cast into the bottomles seas: for by men are we confounded though they by us are sometimes crossed. Our tongues are light because in reprooving men's filthy vices, and our good counsel is termed nipping injury, in that it accords not with their foolish fancies. Our boldnesse rash, for giving Noddies nipping answeres, our dispositions naughtie [wicked] for not agreeing with their vile mindes, and our furie dangerous because it will not beare with their knavish behaviours ... (B3-B3v)

They love to go hansomly in their apparel, and rejoice in the pride thereof, yet who is the cause of it, but our carefulnes, to see that everything about them be curious. Our virginitie makes us virtuous, our conditions courteous, & our chastitie maketh our truenesse of love manifest. They confess we are necessarie, but they would have us likewise evil. (C1v)

At the end of men's fair promises there is a Laberinth, & therefore ever hereafter stop your eares when they protest friendship, lest they come to an end before you are aware whereby you fall without redemption. The path which leadeth thereunto is man's wit, and the miles' ends are marked with these trees: Follie, Vice, Mischiefe, Lust, Deceite & Pride. These to deceive you shall be clothed in the raimentes of Fancie, Vertue, Modestie, Love, Truemeaning, and Handsomeness. Follie will bid you welcome on your way & tel you his fancie, concerning the profite which may come to you by this jorney, and direct you to Vice who is more craftie.... Therefore take heed of it, which you shall doe, if you shun men's flattery, the forerunner of our undoing. (C4v–D1).

Beleeve him not, though he should outsweare you, for although a jade may be still in a stable when his gall backe is healed, yet hee will show himselfe in his kind when he is traveiling: and man's flattery bites secretly, from which I pray God keep you and me too, Amen. (D1)

Honour

From the initial moments of the play when we hear that Don Pedro has 'bestowed much honour' on Claudio (I.i.10) through to Don John's slander made supposedly 'as in love of your brother's honour' (II.ii.33), and to Claudio's accusation of Hero: 'She's but the sign and semblance of her honour' (IV.i.31), it is clear that a sense of honour determines how characters behave in Messina. Masculine and feminine honour are different entities in the play and in early modern England. John

Harington made a common alignment between female honour and chastity, based in humanist discourse:

> A Woman cannot take upon her,
> With beauty, riches, nor with high nobility,
> To claim the true deserved praise of honour,
> If Chastity do fail by her fragility,
> This is the virtue that defends her honour

(Albott, 1600, 27)

For Shakespeare's female characters honour is inherent and embodied, yet simultaneously constituted by public recognition: 'The honor of a maid is her name' Mariana tells Diana as in *All's Well That Ends Well* (III.v.12). Laertes likewise counsels his sister Ophelia that she must 'weigh what loss your honour may sustain' by heeding Hamlet's professions of love, and must on no account lose the 'chaste treasure' of her virginity (*Hamlet* I.iii.29–32). Diana in *All's Well* uses the same jewel metaphor, telling Bertram 'Mine honor's such a ring / My chastity's the jewel of our house / Bequeathed down from many ancestors' (*AWW* IV.ii.45–7). Virginity is, without any need for activity, 'honourable' and its loss is therefore pollution. If Bertram 'fleshes his will in the soil of her honour', Diana will be 'corrupt' (*AWW* III.v.73 and IV.ii.16–17). Shakespeare's narrative poem *The Rape of Lucrece* details how a woman responds to the most violent attack on her honour. Although confident that she is innocent in terms of intent, Lucrece resolves on suicide to sacrifice her polluted body and redeem her honour: "'Tis honor to deprive dishonor'd life, / The one will live, the other being dead'. The Friar's plan for Hero in *Much Ado About Nothing* imitates Lucrece's policy to kill her shame and regenerate her honour through suicide: 'My shame so dead, mine honor is new born' (*Luc.* 1184–90).

'Marriage is an honourable estate' declared the Book of Common Prayer, drawing on St Paul's letter to the Hebrews (Heb.13:4). The marriage service explained that it was an institution honoured by God himself in that it was the first ordinance following the creation, it was instituted in paradise, and that Christ's first miracle had been to turn water into wine at the wedding in Canaan (John 2:1–11). One effect of the Protestant Reformation had been to elevate the importance of chaste marriage, in contrast with Catholicism's exclusive celebration of absolute celibacy. The preacher Henry Smith reminded listeners and readers that St Paul commended not only the honour-able estate of matrimony, but said 'the bed is honourable' too (Smith, 1591, 22). In *Much Ado*, Margaret reiterates this view, teasing Hero 'Is not marriage honourable in a beggar?' (III.iv.28). Given this context, Beatrice and Benedick's antipathy to marriage can be read as spiritually as well as socially aberrant. Don Pedro's determination that they will 'temporize with the hours' (I.i.255) eventually results in Benedick's request to enter the 'state of honourable marriage' with Beatrice at the end of the play.

Masculine honour, traditionally associated with military valour, was by the end of the 16th century, being reconfigured as part of civilian society. The transition from chivalric to courtly honour is marked throughout Shakespeare's work. Hotspur, in *Henry IV Part 1*, who longs to 'pluck bright honour from the pale-faced moon' and rescue 'drowned honour by the locks' (*1 HIV* I.iii.201–207) is romantically anachronistic in comparison to Falstaff's sceptical 'What is honour?' and his conclusion that it is no more than 'air' (*1 HIV* V.i.135).

The potentially explosive effect of channelling the passion of military honour into courtly etiquette is examined in Bernadetto Varchi's *The Blazon of Jealousie* (1615) which noted men's obsession with female chastity as the source of honour, especially in hot countries like the Messina of the play's setting:

> Jealousy commeth in respect of a man's Reputation and Honour, according as his nature is, or as his Breeding hath beene, or after the fashion and manner of the Country, in which he is borne and liveth, … they say, that the Southerne Nations, and such as dwell in hot Regions are very Jealous; eyther because they are much given and inclined unto Love naturally: or else for that they hold it a great disparagement and scandal, to haue their Wives, or their Mistresses tainted with the foul blot of Unchastity: which thing those that are of contrary Regions, and such as live under the North-Pole, take not so deep at the heart.

> (Varchi, 1615, 21)

The opening of *Much Ado* thus sets up a familiar cultural context in which the victorious soldiers are obliged to reconfigure their 'honour' in battle in domestic contexts of dancing and courtship.

John Norden's *The Mirror of Honour* (1597), which addressed soldiers but defined honour in religious terms, spoke precisely to these changed circumstances. He noted that too many 'think it more consonant to their professions, to betake them to more offensive exercises, wherein neither can the God of heauen be glorified, nor their duty in armes truly discharged'. Norden's pamphlet, published the year before the play was composed, forms a striking intertext for the motives guiding Don Pedro, Claudio, Benedick and Don John, which has not previously been noticed by critics:

> For honor is in nothing more gained, then by noble vertues ... For every vertuous and truely praise worthie action, floweth from that valour which is grounded upon that wisdome which both teacheth the way to true honour, and discovereth the infirmitie of such as walke in vaine glorie ... And therefore every man that longeth for honour (as all men for the most part, without flatterie, doe) must foster religion & the religious which procureth honour. In regard whereof, the most honorable person so little respecteth honour, as hee priseth his vttermost trauailes, yea his life, little worth to maintain the same.
>
> (Norden, 1597, 20–21)

As the military commander, Don Pedro takes the lead in promoting what he believes is an honourable course of action in a civilian context: setting up good matches for the soldiers under his care and then acting with what he believes to be wisdom and good government in the crisis raised by Don John's accusations. Borachio plays on the insecurities of the soldiers in this new context. He is confident that the plot will work because the news is given 'as in love of your brother's honour who hath made this match' (II.ii.33–34) and, indeed, Don Pedro claims 'I stand dishonoured' for matching Claudio 'to a common stale' (IV.i.64–65). He vows 'upon mine honour' to have seen her at the window and continues to maintain 'on my honour she was charged with nothing / But what was true and very full of proof' (V.i.104–105). It is Benedick who, having watched the vulnerable Hero collapse, acts with the greater honour (according to Norden's definition) by so little respecting his own honour or reputation with his comrades, as to disregard it in supporting the dishonoured Hero, to the point of challenging Claudio. He shows mature wisdom and judgement by maintaining that Don Pedro and Claudio have 'the very bent of honour' (IV.i.186) in spite of their outrageous conduct in the church.

To a certain degree, their outrage and sense of dishonour is provoked by pride. Norden warns that pride is especially dangerous for 'military men that seem to challenge it as a peculiar badge of their profession, wherein they stand upon their honour (as they seeme) to encounter in arms the proudest in conceit' (Norden, 1597, 22). Norden reminds them that God exalts the meek and '*throweth downe the proude*', pointing out that this sin is 'an infernall poyson' which is anti-social and closely allied to envy (23). He continues that envy 'lurketh in the tents of most valiant souldiers' and 'followeth honour, as a vulture to deuoure it' in others, feeding 'only upon the damnable desire of doing injurie to the best, who in all loue ought to be cherished and fostered, comforted and encouraged in vertue' (24). Norden's words describe precisely the thin motivation of Don John, who wants to feed his own displeasure by injuring 'the most exquisite Claudio' who has become his brother's right-hand man: 'that young start-up hath all the glory of my overthrow. If I can cross him any way, I bless myself every way' (I.iii.46 and 61–63). Don John wishes the cook were of his mind, and would poison the guests at the ball. All 'Commanders', captains and soldiers of true worth hate such perverse passion 'that macerateth it self at the prosperity, and triumpeth at the harmes of other men' Norden points out (24). Don John makes no secret of it, remarking 'it cannot be denied but I am a plain-dealing villain' (I.iii.29–30), something that Don Pedro already knows from his brother's previous military rebellion. Benedick immediately suspects that 'the practice' of the plot 'lives in John the bastard / Whose spirits toil in frame of villanies' (IV.i.188–89).

Don Pedro's failure to recognise the villainy make it clear that the crime and the blame do not rest exclusively with Don John or his envy. The reactions of the older men serve to diffract responsibility between the male characters (except Benedick and the Friar). Leonato feels he is obliged to behave 'like an honourable father' (I.i.105) to protect his own social identity, and first vows to 'tear' Hero limb from limb if her accusers are telling the truth, or to challenge them in her defence 'if they wrong her honour' (IV.i.190–92). In *The Tempest*, Prospero is bound by the same paternal duty, having enslaved Caliban for his more physically violent crime in seeking to 'violate / The honor of my child' (*Tempest* I.ii.348) by rape. When Leonato and Antonio offer to fight Claudio 'despite his nice fence and his active practice' (V.i.75), their age exposes this paternal code of honour to ridicule. John Norden's advice – that, rather than rushing into revenge, 'Let all men consult with reason' and consider whether true valour ought to launch out into 'such vain-glorious attempts' which can often produce a need for repentance (24) – strikes a chord here. Words prove more of an effective challenge after Borachio has confessed and Leonato adopts the same sarcastic tone as Antony in *Julius Caesar* to confront the princes who have supposedly killed his daughter:

> Here stand a pair of honourable men
> A third is fled that had a hand in it.
> I thank you, princes, for my daughter's death;
> Record it with your high and noble deeds.
> 'Twas bravely done, if you bethink you of it.

> (V.i.256–60)

Benedick's understated, earnest challenge is what Norden defines as honourable godly justice 'to protect the innocent … as a hand to hold them vp, a sword to defend them', and 'a buckler to withstand the rigour, cruelty and oppression of the wicked' (24). The appearance of the Constables and the Watch's evidence brings justice in a less violent way but does not undercut Benedick's honourable behaviour which, in turn, assures Beatrice of his love and so compensates for his dishonourable way of winning her heart with 'false dice' in the past (II.i.255–57).

Fashion

Borachio's comment 'seest thou not what a deformed thief this fashion is?' (III.iii.120) draws attention to an immediate material context for the play. Keeping up with fast-changing European styles was a national preoccupation according to writers of the time, so the display of costume on stage in fictional Messina would have doubtless had its own appeal to spectators. Thomas Nashe described England as 'the Players stage of gorgeous attire, the Ape of all Nations' superfluities, the continual Masquer in out-landish habiliments' and warned that the country would be punished for 'wanton disguising thy self against kind, and digressing from the plainness of thine Ancestors' (Nashe, 1593, 150–51). The extracts below indicate something of the cultural context which informs the play's numerous references to clothing, and suggest how actions like Benedick's change from soldier to lover or Margaret's taste in accessories would have resonated in early performances.

(a) Thomas Harrison's account 'Of Their Apparell and Attire' in his description of England formed part of the 1587 version of Holinshed's *Chronicle* (which Shakespeare read), and went into detail:

> The fantastical folly of our nation (even from our courtier to the carter) is such that no form of apparel liketh us longer than the first garment is in the wearing, if it continue so long, and be not laid aside to receive some other trinket newly devised by the fickle-headed tailors, who covet to have several tricks in cutting, thereby to draw fond customers to more expense of money. For my part, I can tell better how to inveigh against this enormity than describe any certainty of our attire; sithence such is our mutability, that today there is none to the Spanish guise, tomorrow the French toys are most fine and delectable, ere long no such apparel as that which is after the high Almain [German] fashion, by and by the Turkish manner is generally best liked of, otherwise the Morisco gowns, the Barbarian sleeues, the mandilion worne to Collie weston ward, and the short French breeches make such a comelie vesture, that except it were a dog in a doublet, you shall not see any so disguised, as are my countrymen of England. And as these fashions are diverse, so likewise it is a world to see the costliness and the curiosity: the excess and the vanity: the pomp and the bravery: the change and the variety: and finally the fickleness and the folly that is in all degrees: insomuch that nothing is more constant in England than inconstancy of attire … Neither will I meddle with our variety of beards, of which some are shaven from the chin like those of Turks, not a few cut short like to the beard of marques Otto, some made round like a rubbing brush, other with a *pique de vant* (O fine fashion!) or now and then suffered to grow long, the barbers being grown to be so cunning in this behalf as the tailors … Some lustie courtiers also and gentlemen of courage, do wear either rings of gold, stones, or pearl in their ears, whereby they imagine the workmanship of God not to be a little amended. But herein they rather disgrace than adorn their persons, as by their niceness in apparel, for which I say most nations doo not unjustly deride us, as also for that we do seem to imitate all nations round about us wherein we be like to the *Polypus* or Chameleon; and thereunto bestow most cost upon our arses, & much more than upon all the rest of our bodies, as women do likewise upon their heads and shoulders.
>
> (1587, 171–72)

Benedick's appearance of 'fancy' in the 'strange disguises' he has adopted follows Harrison's description. As well as visiting the barber and brushing his hat, his changes of costume 'to be a Dutchman today, a Frenchman tomorrow – or in the shape of two countries at once, as a German from the waist downward, all slops, and a

Spaniard from the hip upward, no doublet' (III.ii.29–35) are material evidence that he has turned lover. German style breeches or 'slops' were mocked for their size. Middleton's story of the Ant when he was a Ploughman in *Father Hubbards Tales* (1604), for example, jokes:

> His breeches, a wonder to see, were as full as deep as the middle of winter, or the roadway between London and Winchester, and so large and wide withal that I think within a twelvemonth he might very well put all his lands in them; and then you might imagine they were big enough, when they would outreach a thousand acres.
>
> (Middleton, *Collected Works*, 2007, 157)

Women's delights

Women's delights in masks or vizards, starched ruffs (which also mask the face), headdresses, slit sleeves and large farthingales are satirised in John Marston's, *The Scourge of Villainie* (London, 1598).

> What's in't? some man. *No, nor yet woman kinde,*
> But a celestial Angel, fair refined.
> The devil as soon. Her mask so hinders me
> I cannot see her beauty's deity.
> Now that is off, she is so vizarded,
> So steep'd in Lemons'-juice, so surphuled
> I cannot see her face …
> Her mask, her vizard, her loose-hanging gown
> For her loose lying body, her bright spangled crown
> Her long slit sleeve, stiffe busk [whalebone corset], puffe verdingall
>   [large farthingale],
> Is all that makes her thus angelical.
> Alas, her soul struts round about her neck,
> Her seat of sence is her rebato set,
> Her intellectual is a fained niceness
> Nothing but clothes, & simpering preciseness.
>
> (Marston, 1598, F6–F6v)

Who could wear what

Who could wear what was a matter for national legislation in 1597 with sumptuary laws specifying types of cloth for different social ranks. According to these laws, none except earls and countesses were to wear 'cloth of gold or silver tissued, purple silk' although viscount-esses' kirtles could be gold or silver and knights of the garter could wear purple mantles. Barons and baronesses were allowed to wear silver or cloth of gold mixed or embroidered with gold, silver and pearl. Nobody below the rank of barons' wives and daughters, Maids of Honour, and ladies of the privy chamber or those with an income of less than 500 marks a year were permitted to wear headdresses trimmed with pearl. None below the rank of knights and their wives could wear velvet upper garments, silk embroidery or silk stockings. The eldest sons of knights and their wives were permitted to wear velvet gowns, cloaks, hose, doublets, kirtles. The wives of gentlemen with coats of arms could wear satin, damask, taffeta and grogian. The slippery relationship between clothes and class difference caused concern for writers like the puritan Philip Stubbes, who noted 'Do not both Men and Women (for the most part) everyone in general go attired in silks, velvets, damasks, satins, and what not? which are attire only for the nobility and gentry and not for the other at any hand?' (Stubbes, 1583, sig. A4v). Margaret's adoption of her mistress Hero's clothes to woo at the window, and Dogberry's proud claim to having two gowns are details that capture cultural anxieties about the unstable nature of garments. The play's pattern of sartorial imagery draws attention to the ways in which theatre exemplified and advertised the fluidity of social identity, as something that could be adopted or taken off as easily as a suit of clothes.

Music and dance

Dance and song are important dimensions of the social interaction staged in *Much Ado*. In addition to the two songs included in the script – Balthasar's song in Act III scene ii and the song of mourning at Hero's tomb in Act V scene iii – there are brief allusions to song. Margaret refers to a song and dance called 'Light of Love' (III.iv.40) and Benedick attempts to sing 'The god of love' (V.ii.26–29). Of these, Benedick's song is the only one for which there is a contemporary record. It is by William Elderton, a ballad-writer and actor. After its appearance in 1562, it was imitated and parodied many times, which testifies to its popularity. The original song was discovered in 'The Braye Lute Book' in 1958 as part of the collection of James

M. Osborn. A facsimile is included in Seng, *The Vocal Songs in the Plays of Shakespeare: A Critical History* (1967, 62–63). The song is an interesting intertext since the lyrics of the first verse are echoed in Benedick's wishes and situation in the play. The plot does turn Benedick's sorrowful service in challenging Claudio into joy. As well as referring to the resolution of the merry war, a brawl (his duel) turns into bliss (love from Beatrice) later in this scene with news of the Hero's false accusation. He asks the priest to 'bind me' and he jokes that he will take Beatrice 'for pity' (V.iv.20 and 92–93). The modern transcription of the first verse below is by F.H. Mares and comes from Appendix 3 of his edition of the play.

> The gods of love that sits above
>   and know me, and know me,
>   how sorrowful I do serve,
> grant my request that at the least
>   she show me, she show me,
>   some pity that I deserve;
> that every brawl may turn to bliss
>   to joy with all that joyful is.
>   Do this my dear and bind me
> for ever and ever your own;
>   And as you here do find me
>   so let your love be shown,
> for till I hear this unity
>   I languish in extremity.

> (Mares, 1988, 159)

Dance begins the process of formal courtship in Act II scene i and a dance concludes the whole play, mimicking the process of courtly masques in which the entertainment concluded with the performers selecting partners from the audience to dance with them. The first detailed record of 15th and 16th-century dances is Thoinot Arbeau's *Orchesographie*, published in French in the form of a dialogue in 1589. Ian Payne (2003) gives a useful description of the quadrant pavan such as might be used for the masked ball. A fuller sense of the social importance of dance is conveyed by Bathélemy de Montagut's *Louange De La Danse*, which drew on the traditions established in earlier dance manuals. The extracts below on how to reverence (an action which would have accompanied entrances and exits) and how to dance a galliard (the dance referred to by Beatrice, which followed the pavan) are translated by Barbara Ravelhofer from her edition of the text.

De La Reverence

That is why, having doffed one's hat with the left hand, which one will place casually on the thigh, one should look at the company before one [i.e. the company which enters the room] with modest composure. Then, approaching it, after three or four deliberate steps, one should gently slide the right leg forwards, without bending it at all, until it touches the left which will be bent. Stopping here, with the feet widely turned out, gently bending one [leg] and then the other, one must disengage the left imperceptibly, and do two or three steps in the same way in succession, until one has met those who are entering. And this same action should be followed when one enters oneself to join a group.

(Montagut, 2000, 115–17)

Le Gaillarde

To demonstrate the *gaillarde* well and in a manner easy to follow, first make a *coupe* with the last step of the right foot to catch the *cadence*, so as to begin with the same foot [the right]; having bent the knees a little, on which *plié* jump onto the ball of the left foot, the legs well stretched, and move sideways on tiptoe with the right while turning; then slide the left foot, also on the toes, close to the right, without bending for the *chasse*. But, most importantly, be well advised; note that in this movement the right foot, which is in front, must be lifted as soon as the left [joins it], and that at the same time as one keeps it in the air, one must, while jumping, change foot, lifting the left, then making a *coupe* with it, bringing it forwards in order to disengage gently the right which is behind; do all this before bending the knees only when getting back into the initial position.

(Montagut, 2000, 151)

4 Key Productions

Theatrical interpretations of *Much Ado About Nothing* have ranged from minimalist stagings like Edward Gordon Craig's 1903 touring production through to the extravagant, pictorial grandeur of Henry Irving's in 1882 which also toured in Britain and America, running for a record 212 consecutive performances. Irving employed over 600 people for his production and, in line with Victorian theatrical traditions, placed heavy emphasis on spectacle. The church scene was the crowning glory of the production. Percy Fitzgerald noted 'the art displayed here, the combination of "built up" scenery with "cloths", the rich harmonious tintings, the ecclesiastical details, the metal-work, altars, etc. made an exquisite picture'. The stage picture was itself the subject of a picture, and later an engraving of the scene by Forbes–Robertson who played Claudio. Actors entered to the resonant tones of the organ and represented a large group of clerics carrying censers and candles and wedding guests in addition to the protagonists. Fitzgerald argued that the state and publicity of the scene, the crowds and rich dresses and ecclesiastical robes, brought out 'the "distressful" character of such a trial for a young bride' (Fitzgerald, 1893, 193). Some critics were less complimentary, arguing that only the excellent acting of the principals and the ensemble managed to rescue the show from being 'over-weighted with upholstery and wardrobe' (*Sunday Times*, 15 October 1882). The play's concern with fashion and appearances has continued to inspire ornate visual designs, however, as in the American productions of Daly and Sothern (1896, 1904–05, 1911 and 1913), through to Douglas Seale (1958), and latterly James Edmondson's for the Oregon Shakespeare Festival (1976). Edmondson's and Terry Hands's (1982) productions both used costume and set to critique a society obsessed with superficial appearances. The same idea informed David Nicholls's *Shakespeare Re-Told* (2005), an adaptation set in a television studio.

Full details of the play's varied stage history can be found in John Cox's *Shakespeare in Production* (1997) edition of the play. Pamela Mason's shorter *Text and Performance: Much Ado About Nothing* (1992) gives an account of four productions: the fairy-tale style of John Gielgud's postwar Royal Shakespeare Company show which ran for ten years from 1949; the festive mode of Zeffirelli's 1965 National Theatre production, set in Sicily; the return to a high Renaissance setting, a fuller text and a darker interpretation by Trevor Nunn and the RSC in 1968; the use of a Colonial Indian setting in John Barton's 1976 RSC production in which Barton made an interestingly original, though controversial, decision to present Dogberry (played by John Woodvine) as an Anglo-Indian who was very proud of his English but whose command of the language was far from perfect. Mason's book concludes with a brief survey of performance in the 1980s, including a valuable reading of the Renaissance Theatre Company's inaugural season's production at Birmingham Repertory Studio in 1988, directed by Judi Dench.

Rather than attempt a survey of interpretations, the present book selects six British and North American productions to illustrate how the text has been realised via different approaches and media. It begins by focusing on two relatively neglected stage productions with contrasting styles. The following chapter begins with the analyses of two more stage productions that were adapted for television: Zeffirelli's in 1965–67 and Joseph Papp's 1972 New York Shakespeare Festival production. It concludes by considering a performance made specifically for television by the BBC (1984) and a film version directed by Kenneth Branagh (1993).

Tragical-comical-historical-pastoral: RSC (1990)

Bill Alexander's Royal Shakespeare Company production successfully brought together an early modern design and a cultural preoccupation with gender that had become increasingly prominent through the 1980s. The lights came up on a country garden setting designed by Kit Surrey which, as Paul Taylor noted, looked 'as though it might well come under the auspices of the National Trust' (*Independent* 12 April 1990). The broad sweep of hedges, the arbours, seats and garden swing radiated affluence, leisure and a complacent sense of harmony. This was no Merchant/Ivory production with ladies twirling parasols, however. The action opened on Beatrice (played by Susan Fleetwood) fencing with Leonato, triumphantly winning the bout with a palpable hit and flexing her rapier at the same time as her razor-sharp wit in dialogue with the messenger. Her sword-play, along with the shouting of lines like 'how many hath he killed', made it clear that Beatrice was not cast in the conventional model of early modern womanhood, even though she was dressed in rich 17th-century costume. The first impression was of a powerful, complex and determined individual who would be more than a match for 'Signor Mountanto' in any skirmish of wit. Beatrice threateningly put her sword under Benedick's chin for the line 'Scratching could not make it worse and 'twere such a face as yours were' (I.i.101–2) and threw down her gauntlet on her exit at 'You always end with a jade's trick. I know you of old' (I.i.139). Gauntlets were a trope of the battle of the sexes, a marked change from previous productions like Trevor Nunn's in 1968 where they were exclusively male props symbolising masculine honour (Mason, 1992, 60). The impossibility of containing such violent passions in the boundaries assigned by gender or by peace was clear. The potential for war was already tangible in the enclosed garden.

The arrival of Don Pedro and his party produced a gendered division of the stage. The prompt book makes repeated references to 'the girls' as a group. While Beatrice retreated to a seat down stage left, close to Hero, Don Pedro and the soldiers grouped together stage right in what the prompt book calls the 'locker-room' (RSC/SM/1/1990/MC2). Leonato presented Don Pedro a 'loving cup' of wine, which was passed round the group: Don Pedro to Claudio, to Benedick, a servant and to Conrade, who returned it to Don Pedro. The male chain of 'loving' and communion thus significantly excluded Don John. The imminent collapse of the locker-room was marked when Don Pedro noticed Hero, took off his hat, regretfully, on the line 'I think this is your daughter', and then turned to remove his military cloak and wash. When Don Pedro professed Leonato's welcome was genuine – 'I dare swear he is no hypocrite but prays from his heart' – there was a glimpse of Beatrice's ability 'to see a church by daylight' and perceive Don Pedro's own well-hidden discomfort, before she bowed. Don Pedro's high social status was subtly undercut in John Carlisle's fine performance by a deep sense of loneliness.

Michael Billington pointed out 'This is no princely philosopher but an ageing Cavalier, shrouded in solitude and hungry for emotional contact' (*Guardian*, 12 April 1990). Charles Osborne identified 'hidden depths of feeling in several directions' in a fascinating 'portrait of Elizabethan sexual ambiguity' (*Daily Telegraph*, 12 April 1990). When Claudio (John McAndrew) knelt to ask Don Pedro 'your highness now may do me good' and kissed Don Pedro's hand, Carlisle did not go as far as stroking Claudio's cheek (as had happened in Hands's 1985 production), but gave full weight to the promise to learn 'any hard lesson that may do thee good' (I.i.274). He broke off Claudio's musings over Hero with the words 'Look what will serve is fit' with a bluff expression that nevertheless betrayed the fact that it was too painful for him to hear any more.

Cavalier-style costumes for both men and women deftly material-ised the text's imagery relating to fashion, as exemplified in Benedick's comment 'the body of your discourse is sometime guarded with frag-ments, and the guards are but slightly basted on neither' (I.i.266–8). This was a society fond of displaying its material wealth quite literally in terms of weighty, rich fabrics, decorations and accessories. Benedick (played by Roger Allam) kissed his hand at 'and so I leave you' in a parody of courtly manners that mocked Claudio's new romantic motley. However, the 'deformed thief' who 'turns about all the hot-bloods between fourteen and five and thirty' (III.iii.126–8) showed his influence most strongly when Benedick turned from soldier to lover and reappeared after the overhearing scene wearing a jacket and breeches in pale green shot silk, with pale pink trimmings. Allam's Benedick seemed to be the grotesque personification himself as he had considerable difficulty stealing out of his friends' company in his decorated, courtly shoes. By emphasising a social preoccupation with conspicuous wealth in the form of clothes, the production spoke *for* the cultural world of 1590s England in which, according to commenta-tors of the time, the fast-changing fashions led many people to exceed the limits of sumptuary laws and of their own purses (see Chapter 3). It spoke equally immediately *to* the sensibilities of British spectators influenced by 'new romantic' and yuppie culture through the 1980s.

Lighting played a key part in identifying changes of locale since the set remained the same throughout with small pieces of furni-ture (a chandelier or curtains) flown in to indicate an interior scene. Lighting suggested time of day, as would have been the case in a 1590s production using torches or candles. In 1990, the overhearing scenes took place in bright, hot sunshine of noon in the garden while, at the end of Act I scene i, Antonio and Leonato entered in semi-darkness to consider what the servant had overheard. Light thus became a visual metaphor for characters' ability to see, to be emotionally exposed or secretive, and to suggest mood. It was no accident that 'all Don John's plottings seem to take place in gathering dusk' as Billington noted (*Guardian*, 12 April 1990). Brian Harris's inspired lighting design brought out what is already implicit in the temporal sequence of the original script. The sun-flooded garden scenes which advanced the Beatrice and Benedick romance were juxtaposed with the benighted machinations of Don John, Borachio and Conrade to show the fragility of Messina's happiness. Don John's refusal to 'fashion a carriage to rob love from any' (I.iii.27) was marked by his darker, more severe Parliamentary-style dress. Like Kit Surrey's set and the costumes, the lighting reminded spectators that the cavalier consumption and leisure enjoyed at Leonato's house depended on the deliberate exclusion of 'others' (in terms of social class, race and sexual orientation). The high hedges of the garden and the dazzling sunshine were all that stood between privileged yuppie fun and the inevitable approach of darkness at the end of each day.

The masked ball and betrothal allowed the actors to develop a complex emotional depth to the characters. It began with Hero pushing Beatrice on a swing, and, in twisting the swing round to set it in a spin, Fleetwood celebrated the fast pace of the cinquepace and 'the girls' excitement at the entrance of the maskers (II.i.54–60). She spoke Beatrice's lines 'He were an excellent man that were made just halfway between him and Benedick' (II.i.6–7) more quietly than her usual pitch, though, hinting at Beatrice's desire even in the midst of her wish to amuse. In interview, Fleetwood commented that playing the character as 'very strong-willed' should not hide other elements: 'Beatrice is fascinating, quick-witted, vulnerable, feels deeply and covers it up, has moments when she is pure joy and wants to fly just for the hell of it. She is delicious and courageous' (*Birmingham Post*, 31 March 1990).

Conversation between Don Pedro and Hero and the other couples was not integrated with dancing in this production. Fleetwood gave an aggressive edge to Beatrice's dominance in the conversation with Benedick by slapping his hand at 'I will leave them at the next turning' and running off rather than dancing with him (II.i.140). Benedick's reaction was to exaggerate his chosen role as a confirmed bachelor. He parodied his own addiction to the military life by accompanying his jokes about Claudio wearing the garland 'About your neck, like an usurer's chain / Or under your arm like a lieutenant's scarf' (II. i.177) by miming a military march (promptbook). Allam's Benedick assumed that Don Pedro had betrayed Claudio, giving a bitterness to his comments about the schoolboy stealing the bird's nest (II. i.203–11). Carlisle's Don Pedro let this hang, with a long pause, before verbally conceding Hero to Claudio (or vice versa). The ongoing betrothal negotiations implicitly increased the pressure on Beatrice and Benedick to provide an alternative comic performance. Joking about Beatrice's insults, Benedick pointedly told Hero 'I would not marry her, though she were endowed with all that Adam had left him before he transgressed' (II.i.229–31). Beatrice entered on 'the infernal Ate in good apparel' (II.i.234) and so did not hear the refusal but was, as Benedick knew, fully aware of his following lines. Beatrice's satiric applause at the end of his mock-chivalric appeal to the Prince for a remote quest to avoid 'my Lady Tongue' was the last straw (II.i.252). Exasperated to a degree that suggested he was hurt, Allam threw down the gauntlet which Beatrice had cast to the ground at the end of the first bout of wit, before making his exit.

By playing with the gauntlet at 'thus goes every one to the world but I' (II.i.292–3), Fleetwood signalled Beatrice's sense of isolation. Her reaction to Don Pedro's proposal was just as cruel as her treatment of Benedick though. It was a direct snub, which had its desired effect in ridiculing Don Pedro. She left a long pause after his proposal and then deliberately turned away. John Carlisle played his reaction as shamed and hurt, bodying forth a shadow of Benedick's disguised sensitivity. That Beatrice's brusque independence was no more than a fragile performance was revealed when she turned to the audience, ironically the safest direction to address her confidence that 'my mother cried, but then there was a star danced, and under that was I born'. Paul Taylor noted 'she gives the word an effortlessly bright and explosive emphasis, as though confessing that her own show of gaiety is, like the star's, more a matter of will and pluck than of construction' (*Independent* 12 April 1990). Fleetwood exited with many curtsies, in recognition that Beatrice had caused offence.

The eventual betrothal of Claudio and Hero also caught the tone of embarrassment that characterises much of this scene. At Claudio's line 'Silence is the perfectest herald of joy' (II.i.281), Hero (played by Alex Kingston) visibly jumped on the word 'silence' as though fearing that Claudio was refusing to proceed with the betrothal and accept her, thus pointing up a parallel with his 'no' at the wedding. Don John moved across the back of the stage during the proposal as if to curse it with foreboding. Beatrice's command 'let him not speak neither' prompted the characters to touch hands but they did not kiss. The need to pay very careful attention to etiquette was signalled when Leonato had to quickly amend his response to Don Pedro's suggestion that Beatrice would make an excellent wife to Benedick. Having exclaimed 'Oh Lord', in disbelief, he addressed Don Pedro with extreme deference as 'my lord', in a hasty attempt to reestablish the Prince's status after the latter's rejection by Beatrice.

Since this was a Messina where maintaining appearances was important, it was not surprising that characters often found it easier to speak to the audience than to each other. Claudio walked away from Don Pedro to the front of the stage to express his desire for the wedding to come more quickly. Don Pedro, in turn, returned to a droll and witty role to disguise his hurt, moving downstage to announce 'Cupid is no longer an archer, his glory shall be ours' (II. i.356–57). For all its pastoral leisure, this was a society in which one could not afford to lose face. The following scene presented Don John kneeling at the front of the stage, and shouting his lines of frustration. The *platea* or downstage area was, in early modern terms, a highly appropriate place for a bastard character, legally and culturally marginalised from legitimate society. In Alexander's production, the fact that legitimate characters made similar moves to the *platea* was effective in suggesting that Don John, the cardboard villain, was a scapegoat for the isolation and potentially anti-social impulses held by all the other characters.

The pressure to conceal anything that society might regard as weakness or non-conformity to its projected image of success informed the overhearing scenes. For Act II scene iii a large, phallic tree that matched the clear-cut topiary of the hedges, was flown in centre stage and it was in this that Benedick hid himself, having sent off the boy to get his book. The plotters grouped themselves on a bench that ran round the bottom of the tree trunk. Their physical proximity made it easy for Leonato to cover by a pretence of whispering when he was lost for words at 'How, how I pray you' (II.iii.114).

Benedick's facial reactions could be seen via a small opening in the greenery just above the bench. His emotional responses to the news of Beatrice's affection were signalled by effusions of cigar smoke from inside the tree. As Paul Taylor remarked, throughout the production Allam's cigar was 'a literal smoke screen for the much more sensitive and thoughtful figure he is'. At the same time, the tree graphically advertised the 'fleshy imaginings' of Roger Allam's Benedick as he contemplated the prospect of him and Beatrice between the sheets. Whenever he heard Beatrice's name linked to his own, he spluttered, sending out clouds of smoke which showed the unsettling effect of his own sexual arousal. The precariousness of his hiding place produced some farcical moments when he noticed the return of the boy with his book, and fell down from his perch in the tree as he heard the symptoms of Beatrice's passion (II.iii.145–47).

The plotters ran off like excited schoolboys and their teasing continued in Act III scene ii, making it easy to see why the confirmed bachelor might wish to conceal his feelings. Allam commented that Benedick was in danger of turning into Toby Belch (a role he had played in 1987). The scene featured a more overt sexual reference in the form of a game of coits. Claudio moved to the pole and sat with it between his legs when reporting that Beatrice loved Benedick 'and dies for him' (III.ii.50). At the end of Act II scene iii, once he was alone on stage, Allam's Benedick emerged from the tree in a state of excited confusion. Determination to be 'horribly' in love with Beatrice was addressed to himself, before he reasoned with the audience that 'a man loves the meat in his youth that he cannot endure in his age' (III. ii.130–1) The audience were invited to mock his vulnerability when he sighed and smiled in silence at Beatrice's entrance and her abrupt 'Against my will I am sent to bid you come in to dinner' (II.iii.239). However, his stillness suggested growing confidence and higher status in contrast to her impatience to leave the stage and her shouted line 'I would not have come' (II.iii.242–43). Allam's Benedick responded by shouting 'there's a double meaning in that' and leapt into the air with joy after his final line 'I will go get her picture' (II.iii.254).

His performance effectively brought out the idea that love was a genuine release of emotions that had been suppressed in the military locker room and in a society based on image and the maintenance of image. It spoke to insecurities about masculinity that were, arguably, part of the texture of original performances in late Elizabethan

England where years of peacetime and female rule had disenfranchised traditional concepts of manhood. In Britain in 1990, after 12 years of government by Margaret Thatcher, who emasculated heavy industry even while tactically building up the police and armed forces, definitions of masculinity were similarly in flux. Bill Alexander's production spoke more broadly to a 1990s culture where feminist agendas had gained authority, but by prioritising male bonding it also demonstrated the very real limits to that authority. In Act III scene ii Allam's costume change from a solider to a courtly lover effectively exhibited the full flowering of his new identity and the emotional precariousness that went with it, especially in the difficulty he had in balancing on his high heeled, courtly shoes. Benedick's attempts to conceal himself by lying down, covering his face with his handkerchief and complaining of the toothache were funny and sympathetic in the light of Don Pedro's cruelly droll teasing. His exit with Leonato was painfully slow because of the high heels, and so undercut his verbal attempt to rise above the 'hobby-horses' (III.ii.66).

The emotional journey undertaken by Susan Fleetwood's Beatrice was no less traumatic. In Act III scene i she put her head over the tall hedge and then hid against the proscenium arch, in full view of Hero and Ursula who enjoyed their roles as conspirators. They ran, jumped and laughed in contrast to Beatrice's static, increasingly troubled pose. Beatrice was upset to hear that her companions felt she was incapable of love. The interview effectively undermined her image as a strong iron lady in both ideological and emotional terms and she ended up putting her handkerchief over her head. There was a long pause after her question 'Stand I condemned for pride and scorn so much?' as if she were interrogating the last 20 years of feminism. Darkness closed in as she pronounced 'Contempt, farewell, and maiden pride, adieu / No glory lives behind the back of such' (III. ii.108–110). Having rejected her former assertive independence as ultimately arid in its brittle glory, Fleetwood's Beatrice placed much emphasis on the words 'holy band' and thoughts of a wedding ring on her finger, putting her hands together in prayer. She gasped the last line to show excitement at the thought of being partnered with Benedick, and swelling music heightened the emotional climax on which the first half of the performance concluded.

The church scene represented a further stage in Beatrice's self-redefinition when Fleetwood's character realised the limitations of her power. For all her furious rage at her cousin's betrayal, she was forced to recognise her impotence. When she stepped forward to attack Leonato on the line 'Oh on my soul my cousin is belied' (IV. i.146), Benedick stopped her. She spoke the words 'Oh that I were a man' quietly and sadly. Although her voice rose to a shout in a rage that was 'furious and frightening' (*Financial Times*, 12 April 1990) against Claudio's 'public accusation, uncovered slander, unmitigated rancour' and again at 'manhood is melted into curtsies, valour into compliment', it included a bitter realisation of the futility of her anger. She protested her frustration – 'I cannot be a man with wishing' – with clenched fists, as though recognising the glass ceiling she had come up against (IV.i.302–321). 'Kill Claudio' was played 'tearful and tense to a breathlessly silent house', as Martin Hoyle remarked (*Financial Times*, 12 April 1990). In the subsequent scenes their relationship developed subtly: Benedick referring back playfully to the merry war with reference to the glove she had thrown down in the challenge (V.ii.56). They were blocked opposite each other for a final stand-off in the last scene until all the actors on stage produced love sonnets from their pockets, which Allam and Fleetwood hurried to collect. Public exposure – as lover or as a silenced woman – were no longer important as Benedick stopped Beatrice's mouth in a kiss so long that the other characters onstage eventually turned away in embarrassment. Not even Don Pedro's 'How dost thou Benedick, the married man?' could break it for some moments. In return Beatrice stopped Benedick's mouth with a kiss at (V.iv.114) in order to prevent a quarrel with Claudio.

The harmonious union of these new romantics celebrated love's ultimate triumph over individualism. However emotionally gratifying, it was unsatisfactory in ideological terms. The production never really knew what to do with Fleetwood's assertive Beatrice. Peter Holland remarks that her difference 'was endlessly compromised by the production's self-congratulatory and comforting return to a fascination with the difficulties of masculinity' (Holland, 1997, 36). Perhaps this was exactly the point: Fleetwood's Beatrice enacted the experience of women coming up against the glass ceiling in the 1980s. Her fate is symptomatic of difficulties in dealing with Beatrice's role that stretch back to the Victorian period and forward to the present. Karin Henkel's 2010 German production *Viel Lärm Um Nichts* at the Schauspielhaus, Zurich, took a radical feminist approach by setting the play in a girls' dancing school with the motto 'the world must be peopled'. Beatrice (Carolin Conrad) resisted every attempt to dragoon her into joining the troupe of dancers who rehearsed for the grand spectacle of Hero's wedding, and for their own roles as wives. The fate of Hero (Klara Manzel) in this production magnified Beatrice's fears about marriage. Having descended spectacularly from the skies as a bride only to be rejected by Claudio, Hero's lifeless form was reattached to a trapeze and hauled up above the stage, and then lowered again as a corpse for the second wedding. The production ended with Beatrice struggling to get out of the wedding dress the others tried to force her into. Although Leonato says he hopes to see Beatrice 'fitted with a husband' (II.i.50), this extreme interpretation forced *Much Ado* into an ideological straightjacket that did not fit with the text. It was adaptation rather than translation of Shakespeare's play.

Modernist style: Birmingham Repertory Theatre (1919–20)

In a speech given in 1920, Sir Barry Jackson argued against historical authenticity as metaphorically 'surrounding a live and vital thing with a shroud. If the artist of today is to be of value his work must be visionary of today and tomorrow and not of yesterday' (cited in Cochrane, 1993, 99). Jackson's production of *Much Ado About Nothing* staged in May 1919 and revived in May 1920 at the Birmingham Repertory Theatre, was produced on these principles, sweeping away both the late Victorian fashion for realism and William Poel's experiments in Elizabethan staging in favour of a modernist, stylised design in which the non-verbal elements of sound, movement and colour were tuned into the play's poetic mood. The text was played with very few cuts. *The Birmingham Post* commended Jackson's 'rare faculty of seeing Shakespeare steadily, and seeing Shakespeare whole', noting Jackson's attention to 'the essentials at their true theatrical value' in this production (*Birmingham Post*, 17 May 1920). The company was praised for embodying the 'new blood' which was 'doing more for the advance of the English stage than many a London one of far greater riches and fame' ('Plays Produced').

What Jackson referred to as the 'composite art' of theatre was based on principles of simplicity in line and tone since 'colour and pattern are capable of ruining plays and players' (Cochrane, 1993, 35). For *Much Ado*, the stage decorations designed by Guy Kortright and Jackson consisted of bold black, red and yellow costumes against a black and white set with a choice of red or white flies (curtains) at the back of the stage. The *Birmingham Post* commented: 'The staging is simple almost to audacity. The Medieval costumes are sumptuous' (17 May 1920). Jackson had originally imagined the play in the image of a Veronese painting with 'stiff whale boned dresses and ruffs' but historical accuracy was abandoned in favour of clothes with much cleaner lines whose 'angularity' materialised the play's aesthetic in symbolic ways (Cochrane, 1993, 68). The men's tunics, the women's tightly fitting tabards, and the long hanging false sleeves and high collars successfully conveyed the brittle polish of Messina's social world.

Jackson wrote that the contrasting colours of set and costume 'gave an effect of hard brilliancy which seemed to reproduce entirely the atmosphere of the play with its keen dazzling wit, and the sharp distinction between good and evil characters'. Don John's villainy was marked by a red backcloth as well as a black and yellow costume that made him appear wasp-like, especially as he fastened threateningly on Borachio's shoulder at 'I will endeavour *any thing*' ((II.ii.27–8), emphasis added in promptbook Birmingham Repertory Theatre Archive, Birmingham Central Library). Although Jackson does not specifically refer to yellow as a colour associated with jealousy, Beatrice's reference to Claudio as 'civil as an orange and something of that jealous complexion' (II.i.270–1) may have informed the design since Jackson stresses the importance of 'a feeling for the emotional and symbolic values of colour' in costume design (Jackson, 1928, 68–69). The modernity of Beatrice's unconventional ideas and outspoken manner was sharply defined in the costume designed for Margaret Chatwin, who had previously played the independent Katherina in *The Taming of the Shrew*. A production photograph pictures Chatwin's Beatrice standing arms akimbo as if to challenge the viewer. Her striped bodice, pointed long hanging sleeves and a full skirt with a print of harpies, wings outstretched, all give the strong impression that her every word would indeed stab.

Jackson's design poetics owed much to the experiments of Edward Gordon Craig whose 1903 production of *Much Ado* had toured to Birmingham. In a revolutionary departure from the realism of productions like Irving's, Craig's design used only curtains and light. Count Kessler, who saw the production, commented on the 'strong ray of sunlight, falling on the stage in a thousand colours through an invisible stained-glass window'. The design's comparatively severe minimalism heightened the iconic power of the vast altar and huge crucifix centre stage. Coloured light fell onto the cross, lighting up its colours (Leeper, 1948, 8). Jackson later remarked: 'Here was that impressive simplicity of design that is achieved only by means of impeccable taste', praising the use of light as 'a miracle of beauty I have never seen surpassed' (Jackson, 1955, 77). As Claire Cochrane remarks, Craig's formula of using a single piece of scenery through which to focus the audience's imagination was one taken up in Jackson's early work for the Birmingham Rep (Cochrane, 1993, 35). In *Much Ado*, the action was centred on a raised porch or loggia with a flight of six steps down to stage level, an arch above and balustraded areas to each side with block seats on the stage area below. More steps led down at the back as up-stage exits. A reviewer of the performance on 15 May 1920 (attended by a conference of Esperanto speakers), remarked:

> The setting was as unique as it was simple and pleasing. It consisted of a back cloth of white, a raised platform from the back to the centre of the stage, pillars on either side of the stage, with square boxes which could be used as seats, and a sort of palisading running from these to the wings. The whole of the scenery was of white, with a flooring of black and white squares, and it was a revelation to old theatre lovers like myself to find what wonderful and adequate effects could be secured by such simple means when combined with suitable lighting arrangements.
>
> (Scrapbook 1917–20)

The production used hard, brilliant light which picked out the sharpness of line in the design, giving material shape to what the director Conal O'Riordan saw as a 'crystalline' quality to the humour of *Much Ado* (Cochrane, 1993, 68). The chequered flooring of the stage and the platform area created the effect of pieces moving across a chessboard. In the betrothal of Claudio and Hero, it emphasised Don Pedro's manipulation of events and the cold formality of the situation. Don Pedro (played by Jackson) placed himself between Hero and Claudio when he announced 'I have wooed in thy name', and Claudio was obliged to address his lines 'Lady as you are mine,

I am yours' across Don Pedro's dominant physical presence (II.i.274 and 282–3). Only after Beatrice intervened again did Don Pedro move Claudio in front of him and cross to Beatrice (promptbook) for 'In faith, lady, you have a merry heart' (II.i.287). Pauses punctuated the lines following Don Pedro's proposal, suggesting a lengthy process of rejection. Don Pedro's status as a bachelor had been highlighted in the opening scene by giving him an early entrance to the top of the steps at Benedick's joke 'Shall I never see a bachelor of three score again?' (I.i.187–88). The prompt book notes 'Claudio makes as if to praise Hero to Ben who seeing Pedro stops him' with the line 'Look; Don Pedro is returned … ' (I.i.190). The prompt book offers no more clues about the nature of Don Pedro and Claudio's relationship except for cutting Leonato from the opening of II.iii, thus making a potentially intimate moment of their listening to 'Sigh No More, Ladies'.

Under the direction by Conal O'Riordan, the flight of steps which was the central architectural feature of the set provided a brilliant way of charting the changing relationships between characters in terms of status, intimacy or distance. Movements up or down the steps telegraphed the emotional dynamics in a scene. At the opening, for example, Hero's romantic interest in the 'Young Florentine called Claudio' (I.i.10) was shown by running down the steps to look over her father's shoulder at the letter. In contrast, Beatrice expressed a much more aloof attitude to Benedick by speaking from the balustrade above to ask the messenger whether 'signor Mountanto' was returned (I.i.29). She literally talked down to Benedick from the balustrade at 'I wonder you will be still talking', while he jumped onto the block seat below to challenge her with 'It is certain I am loved of all ladies'. His apparent surrender, jumping to the stage to join the others at 'a God's name I have done', left Beatrice marooned in the upper area and she was forced to climb down the steps as she complained 'You always end with a jade's trick' (I.i.110–39). Their stand-off in the final scene concluded with Benedick jumping athletically from the seat over the balustrade to Beatrice on the upper platform. A reviewer noted that the Beatrice and Benedick scenes were 'of the richest humour' (Scrapbook 1917–20). The ups and downs of their tempestuous relationship were a flirtatious dance up and down the steps.

The erotic nature of movement across the steps was brought out most fully in the ball scene. The musicians and maskers entered from the back of the stage in pairs led by Don Pedro and, interestingly, Don John, and mingled on the raised area at the top of steps. Couples descended from the main group to converse flirtatiously on the steps and then return. A trumpet sounded for the dance proper, which was accompanied by an orchestral rendition of 16th and 17th-century 'old folk dances'. The actors moved in the figure of a chain in a striking, mimetic tableau of what this scene stages: emotional confusion as formal wooing breaks down. The prompt book gives meticulous directions:

> The gentlemen face down stage the ladies face up stage. Don P. leads them from R to L and from L to R alternately on the steps to the bottom of the steps and then out through R.I.E. and back again through R2E. This is done 3 times. The second time every other step is taken for a movement across from R to L or L to R and the pace slightly accelerated. The third time it develops into a romp, the chain breaking in many places. As the remaining end of the chain consisting of Claudio, Marg. and Bor. begin to desend [*sic*] steps Don J. who has been leaning against L pillar on top of steps during the dance, steps suddenly between Marg. and Bor.

While Don Pedro physically inaugurated the social chain, Don John broke it, intervening to sow doubt into Claudio's mind. Don John's disruptive influence had already been shown kinaesthetically at his exit from the first scene where he followed Don Pedro and Leonato, hand in hand, and 'on his way claims Hero, who is talking to Claudio at foot of steps' (promptbook). Claudio responded to this rude gesture by looking after them.

The flight of steps created an ideal platform for more formal tableaux in the wedding scene, the courtroom and the final resurrection scene. Jackson argued that the producer and designer would 'have in mind certain groupings and pictures which will occur at striking moments of the play, and which can only be realised if the same artist has directed the whole' (Jackson, 1928, 69). Stasis marked moments of solemnity and potential tragedy in the production. Claudio paused 'thunderstruck' once Don John delivered his news in III.ii and Hero's lines 'My heart is exceeding heavy' carried extra weight after she had prayed motionless, to the sound of an angelus bell. The church scene maximised the impact of Hero's fall by displaying the bridal party in front of the altar (at the back of the raised platform) and down the steps stage right. The groom's party made their accusations from the main stage level, stage left of the altar, with Benedick furthest downstage, demonstrating his separation from the others. For all its simplicity 'the scene in the church where Claudio denounces the innocent Hero is one which is intensely touching and impressive', a reviewer commented (Scrapbook 1917–20). It was charged with barely contained violence. After Don John had made his accusations and prepared to lead the others off, he was stopped by Benedick, who put his hand under Don John's chin and looked him full in the eyes. This visual reminder of the real villain shifted condemnation away from Claudio. When Don John dropped the sweetmeat box he was holding and ran off, Benedick threw the box after him. Chatwin delivered the line 'Kill Claudio' 'Turning to Ben[edick] fiercely', caus- ing him to move backwards in shock as he said 'Ha! Not for the wide world' (promptbook). The subsequent exchange included some lengthy pauses in contrast to their previously deft movements up and down the steps, signalling the change in their relationship before they went their separate ways.

The courtroom tableau provided a humorous counterpoint to the church scene. Dogberry, Verges, the Sexton, the First Watch, Borachio, the Second Watch, Conrade and the Third Watch all lined up with due ceremony on the raised platform under the archway, but proceedings were comically delayed by the business of passing a cushion and stool along the line from left to right for the Sexton. The deadlock between the Princes and Leonato and Antonio in V.i was staged to create a tragicomic effect. Leonato (played by Frank Moore) created a sense of threat by descending step by step towards them, only to be upstaged when Antonio rushed precipitately 'down to bottom of steps' in front of him to face Don Pedro (promptbook). The wrongdoers Margaret and Borachio seem to have retained a rather sinister power in this scene. Margaret waved her handkerchief at Borachio, who 'look[ed] back at her meaningly and nod[ded] almost imperceptibly', before protesting her innocence. Margaret remained in a dominant position at the top of the stairs once the others exited, and then came down the steps to ask Benedick to write her a sonnet.

The flight of steps (like the early modern stage's galleries) was practically useful for staging the many moments of overhearing. Don Pedro and Claudio's conversation in Act I scene i was observed first by a servant who came out from the back of the stage to sweep the steps. After Don Pedro produced a ring with which to woo Hero,

Borachio entered and spotted it 'dodging behind [the] back pillar' stage right of the archway. The Watch arranged themselves along the fourth step to overhear Borachio's tale from the stage left seat, and crept down the steps to close in on him. Benedick and Beatrice were both obliged to move side to side of the pillars in 'noting' the comments of their friends. A great deal of crossing and re-crossing by the plotters must have created visual comedy here. A further moment of eavesdropping allowed Beatrice and Benedick to reach a romantic understanding in Act V scene ii. Ursula entered slightly early with her news (V.ii.83), saw them sitting together stage left and 'retire[d] tactfully' so that they could kiss after 'Serve God, love me and mend' (V.ii.85) before she reentered.

The final scene combined tableau and movement. Hero and the ladies were displayed on the upper stage area. Claudio decorously ascended the steps to accept her, in line with the formality of the main plot, whereas Benedick vaulted over the balustrade to Beatrice. Dance reintroduced the fluidity of sexual desire again in what, according to the prompt book, looks like a radical ending. Having led Beatrice down to the fourth step to address Don Pedro, Benedick resumed his position at the top to call for music and danced right (offstage) while Don Pedro began the dance with Beatrice at the centre of the steps. This suggests that Benedick's words 'here's our own hands against our hearts' (V.iv.91–92) might have been spoken as truth for once; that the couple had been tricked into marriage and Clarke-Smith's 'hard veneer of brilliance' as Benedick may have continued to the end. Jackson recognised the dangers of oversimplifying a text by aesthetically pigeonholing its characters, but his production showed how stylisation could sharpen the wit and the cruelty found in *Much Ado*.

5 The Play on Screen

In film or television, the audience is not a living community of spectators who are implicated in the play's processes of noting, overhearing and watching. Nevertheless, screen versions direct the gaze of viewers at scenes which are often not realisable on stage. To explore some effects of screen adaptation in *Much Ado*, this chapter will analyse two television productions adapted from the stage, alongside the BBC TV production directed by Stuart Burge and the Renaissance Theatre Company's 1993 film, directed by Kenneth Branagh.

Sicilian passions from stage to screen: National Theatre (1965–67)

In February 1967, BBC1 screened a two-part televised version of the National Theatre production of *Much Ado* directed by Franco Zeffirelli, starring Maggie Smith and Robert Stephens as Beatrice and Benedick. The production, which had opened two years earlier at the Old Vic, had been controversial from the start because it incorporated over 300 modernisations of the text by Robert Graves. Nevertheless, its energetic realisation of the play in an exuberant, anarchic, Sicilian setting was highly acclaimed and the production toured to Bristol, Nottingham, Stratford, Glasgow and Aberdeen. No copies of the screening seemed to have survived but in September 2010, it was redis-covered in a collection donated to the Library of Congress, Washington, by US National Educational Television and a copy deposited at the British Film Institute. Apparently, Zeffirelli disowned the televised version produced by Cedric Messina; his name does not appear on the credits. Whatever Zeffirelli's objections and the limitations of a short rehearsal period and shooting schedule, the recording does make some use of the television medium and so offers more than simply an invaluable insight into the stage production.

The production's setting, in Sicily, was an ideal locale for the explosive juxtaposition between passion and violence on which the plot depends. Messina was a small, close-knit community eager to celebrate with continental *joie de vivre* and equally fascinated by gossip. In spite of this local, provincial character, however, it was larger than life. The women were dressed like the gaudy sugar dolls used in Sicilian folk festivals, while the soldiers had elements of the Mafia and the tightly regimented uniforms of a dictatorship. The maintenance of honour was fundamental in such a society. Remodelling the stage set as a simple square with colonnades and a raised balcony, and decorating it with lights for the masked ball, lent an air of festive artificiality on television. Some characters spoke with exaggerated Italian accents and moved or posed in histrionic versions of *commedia* farce. Ursula, for example, was a hyperbolic Sicilian mother figure with a large hat and black shawl whose praise of 'Sig-nor Benedick' (II.i.95) was deliberately extravagant. As one review pointed out, 'All the stereotypes, played to the hilt, are present, including a noisy brass band which makes the whole evening a raucous carnival' (Loney, 1967, 93).

A carnival atmosphere was quickly established by the arrival of Don Pedro's party in the town square, celebrated with drums, trumpets and a trombone. Hero presented him a bouquet and Margaret distributed drinks to everyone. At the centre of the celebration, Beatrice and Benedick's battle of wit was conducted with elaborate flourishes of handkerchiefs. Beatrice (Maggie Smith) began with a mock curtsy at 'Courtesy itself must convert to disdain if you come in her presence' but ended by shouting her anger at Benedick (Robert Stephens). When Don Pedro announced they would stay for at least a month, Beatrice fainted dramatically under her gauze handkerchief. Such burlesque performance gave the production an energy that was funny and dangerous.

The television version capitalised on the production's use of 'inanimates' to suggest the claustrophobia of Messina. During the masked ball, live actors posed as statues of Moors holding lamps and moved about the dance floor, displaying their ability to watch, overhear, and illuminate private conversations. They witnessed the betrothal of Hero and Claudio and noted Benedick's complaint, 'Oh she misused me past the endurance of a block … ', which is addressed primarily to Antonio (a person apart from the matchmaking in hand). For the first overhearing scene, Act II scene iii, Miss Freeman and Miss Bourne changed into mermaids and Mr Horn into a Triton, to create a fountain in Leonato's garden. When Benedick boasted 'one woman shall not come in my grace' the mermaids moved and tittered. They swung to the music in the instrumental break between the verses of Balthasar's song, and tittered again when Beatrice exited, impatiently, having called Benedick to dinner. The surprising effect of inanimate objects eavesdropping and reacting to one's behaviour was exaggerated by the small screen. Close-up shots of the fountain gave no clue that the statues were anything but what they seemed so their movement disturbed the passive image on screen, blatantly transgressing television's conventions of realism.

Robert Stephens's performance added to the effect by reaching beyond the screen to include viewers as intimate observers like the inanimates. He had already established a relationship with the television audience through his first soliloquy in Act II scene i, when he started to exit but turned quickly back to the camera to gossip 'but that my Lady Beatrice should know me and not know me ... ' (II.i.186). In Act II scene iii his rhetorical question 'May I be so converted?' was direct to camera, in close-up (II.iii.21). The conspirators crowded very close to Benedick in the confined space between the garden hedges, where their whispering and his farcical attempt to disguise himself with a handkerchief increased the sense of suffocated, explosive emotions. When Benedick retreated to the fountain, the mermaids scrutinised him, putting their faces even closer to his at Don Pedro's line 'I could wish he would modestly examine himself' (II.iii.201), at which one of the inanimates looked directly at him. Benedick emerged from the fountain with the production's love-theme music (by Nino Rota) coming up to full volume by the time he reached 'love me' (II.iii.216). He addressed viewers again in arguing 'it must be requited', and that it was 'no great argument of her folly' (accompanied by an admonitory wag of the finger, II.iii.225–6). The full acknowledgement of his passion for Beatrice was marked by an acknowledgement of the inanimates and, implicitly, the audience of silent television spectators. Benedick excitedly confided 'I will go get her picture' (II.i.254) and shook hands with Mr Horn the triton on the fountain.

Maggie Smith's Beatrice had a less intimate relationship with the camera, but the razor-sharp quality of her wit made her performance

absolutely compelling. She mimed the gesture of slitting her throat
on the line 'just so much as you may take at a knife's point and choke
a daw withal' (II.iii.245–6), echoing the malicious violence of Don
John's earlier appearance in I.iii where he was pictured pulling a bird
to pieces for his own amusement. Act III scene i materialised the
smothered excitement of the previous overhearing scene even more
literally by presenting Hero and Ursula hanging out washing with
Beatrice barely concealed at the other side of the washing line. Having
heard them criticise her disdain and scorn, she came to the end of the
washing line, visibly 'exposed'. A much gentler dimension to Beatrice
was revealed in Maggie Smith's beautifully subtle performance of
the soliloquy in close-up. From being full of concern about the 'pride
and scorn' for which she was reputed, her voice softened into a tender
expression of love for Benedick at 'thou dost deserve' which was
spoken as a whisper with her hand on her cheek. Her sense of wonder
at 'I / Believe it better than reportingly' (III.ii.115–16) was followed by
kissing a statue of a cupid, on which the camera dwelt to end the scene.
The film had already hinted that Beatrice's brilliantly acerbic wit was
no more than a defensive shell in Act II scene i after the betrothal of
Claudio and Hero. When Don Pedro quite aggressively pushed himself
onto Beatrice with his proposal 'Will you have me, lady', she pointed
out firmly 'No, my lord' and excused herself assertively in the words
'I was born to speak all mirth and no matter' (II.i.300–4). Moments
later, however, she shifted to a much gentler voice to contradict his view
that she was born in a merry hour. 'No, sure, my lord,' was quiet, sad and
slow, and her sadness continued in the greeting 'Cousins, God give you
joy'. Leonato's line 'Niece, will you look to those things I told you of' was
a welcome excuse for her to leave, visibly upset (II.i.308–11).

    The camera's focus helped to flesh out an emotional relationship
between Hero (Caroline John) and Claudio (Michael Byrne), who
were both presented as young. In the first scene, Hero registered her
interest in Claudio by coyly dropping a flower for him before turning
to exit, and he rushed over to pick it up and savour its perfume as
he asked Benedick 'did'st thou note the daughter of Signor Leonato?'
(I.i.154). Hero was visibly distressed at the thought of having to accept
Don Pedro as a suitor at the ball. Act II scene i opened with the family
group seated together and the camera focused in on her reaction
when she was told 'well, niece, I trust you will be ruled by your father'
(II. i.38). During the dance, she was whisked out of shot by Don Pedro

to 'speak low if you speak love', as if to point up her helplessness in pursuing her real romantic interests.

Claudio was also vulnerable to the machinations of his elders, though their villainy was telegraphed much more openly when Don John (played by Ronald Pickup) appeared in a ridiculous jester's mask and Borachio used a heavy mock-mafia accent for 'Are you not Signor Benedick' as they closed in on him (II.i.146). Claudio's anger at the apparent betrayal of Don Pedro and Hero effectively blazoned forth the shame of dishonour in this Messina. He was like a wounded schoolboy, and Beatrice's reprimand 'Speak, Count, 'tis your cue' (II. i.280) resembled Maggie Smith's later role as Professor McGonagall scolding a Hogwarts pupil in the *Harry Potter* films. The genuine affection between Claudio and Hero was reestablished when he went down on his knees to propose to her at 'I give away myself for you and dote upon the exchange', and she responded by raising him to his feet and kissing him (II.i.284–5). Even at this moment, Messina's fascination with romantic gossip was irrepressible. The close-up of Hero's face showed her looking over Claudio's shoulder to watch Beatrice flirting with Don Pedro.

Stereotype was most exaggerated with the villains. Don John's malice was established in the opening scene when he locked Leonato's hand in an over-tight grip, producing an 'oo' from observers, and making Don Pedro's comment 'Your hand, Leonato' a matter of concern, rather than a mere pleasantry. In Act I scene iii trombone music comically emphasised the cardboard quality of self-declared villainy, spoken by Pickup in close-up to camera while he pulled a garden bird to pieces. Conrade (Edward Petherbridge) was physically eccentric as a foppish mafia gentleman while Borachio (David Hargreaves) had the heaviest mock accent. The trio engaged in a deft use of slapstick; their series of false exits through the orchard creating the weird effect of Shakespeare as performed by The Marx Brothers. Don John raced off at 'Come, let us thither', followed by Borachio and Conrade, only to return to complete his line 'this may prove food to my displeasure' (II.i.60–1). The business of the false exits was repeated on the next line, and on the third occasion – 'If I can cross him any way, I bless myself every way' – Borachio and Conrade started to make an exit but were stopped by Don John's question 'You are both sure and will assist me?' Don John then outmanoeuvred them again, exiting right away from the screen on 'Let's go prove what's to be done' while they rushed to camera again, expecting another false exit, before manically rushing off with the words 'We'll wait upon your Lordship' (I.iii.69). Pickup showed Don John's sadistic satisfaction at manipulating others by relishing a cup of espresso after having delivered his news to Claudio and Don Pedro.

The Watch (whose number included a young Michael Gambon) appeared in the town square with an opening shot looking down from a statue of a conquistador (played by Mr Horn), which suggested the dominance of strict military rule. Rather than enforcing order, however, the Watch's loud voices and chaotic physical movements, which included difficulty in handling their weapons, caused a riotous disturbance. Dogberry, a small-town Mussolini played by Frank Finlay, presided over all. In a parody of Italian sentimentality over children, the Watch sadly considered the case of the baby who needed to wake its nurse with crying. Meanwhile, lightning and thunder – Don John's signature tunes – reminded spectators of what was going on in the orchard. Borachio and Conrade shared an intimate conversation under an umbrella while the watch spied from behind more umbrellas in the rain. Spectators were not given any confidence that the shallow fools would bring matters to right. Preparing to exercise his full authority as deputy Constable, Seacoal swapped his umbrella for the conquistador statue's sword but then fell over because of its weight. Part I of the television show thus ended with the certainty that things would go from bad to worse, an impression later reinforced by the appearance of a statue of Justice blindfolded at the examination scene.

A mood of carnival festivity, mirroring that in Part I, opened the second part of the television broadcast. In Act III, scene iv, nervousness about the imminent wedding was conveyed through a piece of comic stage business in which Margaret, Hero and Beatrice frantically passed round a hairbrush, coffee cup and mirror during Margaret's long speech. Excitement built with news of Claudio's arrival, and a procession of the band and the wedding party around the 'square' to be congratulated by the townspeople. Hero shook hands and blew kisses while Margaret and Ursula distributed flowers. The church scene opened on another 'inanimate' statue of St Sebastian behind the altar and the entry of a doddering priest, attendants and an enthusiastic young server (Christopher Timothy) amidst candles and a resonant Ave Maria. The wedding party processed formally down the aisle singing, Benedick beside Beatrice rather than with Don Pedro, Claudio and Don John, who took up their places first. As the service began, the camera drew back behind and above St Sebastian to look down on the bride. The arrows in the foreground of the picture moved with the actor's body when Claudio said 'no' and provided burlesque reminders of Hero's sacrifice to male principles of honour in the long, high shots used as Claudio rejected her. The ceremony collapsed into a cacophony of shocked cries, Hero herself objecting angrily: 'Seemed I ever otherwise to you?' (IV.i.54). Bodies crowded the screen and Claudio threatened physical violence. Margaret, who had been presented as a flirt throughout, looked shocked, realising her part, and rushed off from near the pillar with her hands to her face.

At Hero's collapse, Don John prevented Don Pedro and Claudio from turning back and hurried them away from the devastation. Honour was a matter of passionate dispute between Leonato and his daughter until they were silently reconciled by the Friar's suggestion. As they began to exit, Hero's need for emotional comfort led her to run back to Beatrice for a hug. This detail seems to have restored the original stage intention since the move had been recorded but then deleted from the prompt book. Beatrice led her back to her father as a single bell tolled as if for a funeral.

In line with the sombre mood, Beatrice covered her head with a black shawl, once again framed by the arrows in the statue above, and thus implying her vulnerability. Her exchange with Benedick was a combination of subdued sadness and mounting fury and distrust, making excellent use of the opportunities offered by close-up. Most shots foregrounded Beatrice with Benedick behind, over her shoulder. A determined, distant look in Smith's eyes suggested she had already thought of revenge but she acknowledged with quiet sadness and a turn of her head that it was not a task Benedick could perform. Robert Stephens registered his disappointment and sympathy with equal gentleness, yet Smith's Beatrice maintained her defensive position throughout his declaration of love. Framed by her shawl in close-up, she could not look at him as she admitted how completely she loved him. The camera moved in so that her face filled the screen as she paused and finally dared to utter the words 'Kill Claudio'. In contrast to Smith's stillness here, Benedick's shocked reaction produced a flurry of distressed movement. She pulled away angrily on the line 'there is no love in you', marched towards the altar to berate Claudio and, on the verge of tears, expressed a deep sense of hurt in her belief that men were only turned into tongue and could not be trusted.

Having reissued the challenge she resigned herself to feminine grief by throwing her shawl around her. Benedick's face was then fore-grounded as he stopped her and reconsidered. Television allowed for a more muted, intense conclusion to the exchange than the stage pro-duction in which Beatrice had placed Benedick's dagger in his hand and he had sheathed it in consent. In the television version, Benedick accepted the challenge and kissed Beatrice's hand very quietly, demon-strating the seriousness of the commitment in all senses of the word. It was deeply moving.

The strange mixture of styles in the production and the television film effectively brought out the uneasy resolution to the play. Confusion about the seriousness of Antonio, Leonato or Benedick's challenges suffused Act V scene i. Viewers were also challenged when Leonato (Gerald James) sarcastically addressed Claudio and Don Pedro as 'honourable men' (V.i.256), speaking directly to camera. Their decorated shoulders framed the shot, and viewers were implicated in the villainy of Hero's shaming as Leonato raised his hat and asked them to 'Record it with your high and worthy deeds / 'Twas bravely done, if you bethink you of it' (V.i.258–60).

The restoration of Hero, the celebratory mood of the final dance and the long awaited and lengthy kiss between Beatrice and Benedick were still tinged with sadness by the lone figure of Don Pedro. Derek Jacobi, who had taken over the stage role from Albert Finney, played an essentially melancholy Don Pedro who disguised his feelings under a very pronounced Italian accent that seemed in keeping with his military identity. In the first scene he was framed in close-up as Benedick revealed Claudio's romantic interest, and then with Benedick drinking espresso as a pair of confirmed bachelors. The nature of his feelings remained ambiguous: he refused to look at Claudio when surrender-ing Hero, and as he moved to sit next to Beatrice, his proposal to her was physically aggressive. What was unmistakable was the sense of isolation with which the film ended by focusing on him. Amidst Nino Rota's 'love theme' and the gentle lights of the final dance, Don Pedro lit his cigar and then retreated from Leonato's household, waved to by Beatrice and Benedick. He ignored the news of Don John's arrest, continuing to walk away into the square. As the music slowed, a long shot from above framed Don Pedro sitting alone with his cigar and sword under conquistador statue. The bright, gaudy spectacle of carnival had been eclipsed as the screen darkened.

Rough riders return home: New York Shakespeare Festival (1972) and CBS–TV (1973)

Television's ability to construct the realism of domestic life was fully exploited in the screen adaptation of Joseph Papp's 1972 production of *Much Ado* which played first in Central Park, then on Broadway and was televised by CBS to an initial audience of 20 million people. This *Much Ado* was a national story as well as a domestic one. The gulf between polite civilian life and military action that is bridged by the play's opening scene was a topical keynote of the production. Papp remarked 'we are reaching out across the country' in a tale 'set in America at the turn of the [twentieth] century' where the soldiers are returning and 'though the war is over the battle of the sexes goes merrily on'. Don Pedro and his party were cast as Roosevelt's 'Rough Riders' (the First Voluntary division of the US Cavalry returning victorious from battle with the Spanish in Cuba) to be greeted with celebratory mascots and festivals in fashionable New York. Roosevelt's farewell speech to his troops on 15 September 1898 was a 300-year echo of the play, reminding the rough riders that they would have to reintegrate into society and work as hard as everyone else. The play's term 'Signor' was Americanised as 'Captain' in the film to familiarise the soldiers. The film also showed Hero cuddling a teddy bear in her bedroom, a toy that affectionately alluded to Roosevelt as an enthusiastic bear hunter. This detail, just before Claudio brutally rejected her, commented ironically on the naiveté of Roosevelt's idea of demobilisation and domestication, a topic brought out in details of the production.

Leonato's commendation of the victorious captain returning 'with full numbers' (I.i.8–9) rang true in the 1898 context since the rough riders saw few casualties, a pointed contrast to America's heavy losses in the Vietnam war. As the rough riders of Papp's production were greeted with a full marching band, the television audience of 1972 may have recalled Roosevelt's reassurance that 'those who stayed had done their duty precisely as did those who went' diffracted through their immediate experiences of drafting troops for Vietnam. Roosevelt's determination that 'no distinction of any kind was allowed' between those who had seen action and 'those whose harder fate it had been to remain' was again a popular, hotly debated political stance among Americans who regarded the Vietnam war as morally wrong (Roosevelt, 1899, 130).

The design of the production, by Tom John, implicitly addressed the nostalgia of its national audience by alluding to a time of great national confidence, when America established itself as a world power through coast-to-coast settlement and railways, and boasted the largest agricultural and steel output in the world. The setting was domestic: a house with a wooden covered front porch that contrasted markedly with the 'home' in contemporary TV series *The Waltons* (set in the Depression) since every detail from flower arrangements to decanters and carpets advertised the wealth on which America's sense of home was based. Leonato's drawing room featured sumptuous furniture and decorations that framed the protagonists. The small screen was crowded with objects and at some points the mass of detail threatened to make the film, like Irving's production, 'over-weighted with upholstery and wardrobe' (*Sunday Times*, 15 October 1882). However, the very material nature of Claudio and Hero's betrothal was effectively conveyed via these civilised surroundings. The costumes, designed by Theoni V. Aldredge, emphasised an easy, luxurious style of living. The women wore satins, silks and costume jewellery while the men replaced their military uniforms with casual blazers, silk ties and waistcoats, and straw boaters. A barber's shop in which Benedick was discovered in Act III, scene ii was a site of male transformation from soldier to lover. Don John, who remained in his uniform throughout, took control of the Hero–Claudio romance plot by occupying the barber's chair and then shutting up the shop after sowing the seeds of the plot. Earlier Don John and Borachio plotted at a piano, expressing their malevolence via an increasingly angry rendition of 'The Hall of the Mountain King' in duet. A separate bunkhouse used as barracks by Don Pedro and his followers was swept, dusted and redecorated with roses and candles by the love-stricken Benedick in anticipation of Beatrice's arrival in Act V scene ii. The television film's use of fast motion for Benedick's housework pointed to the artificial foundations of the scene, presenting the conversion of war into peaceful hard work and wealth, *pace* Roosevelt's speech, in terms of the American dream.

Music, drink and flowers were significant features of the celebratory atmosphere. Peter Link orchestrated a mixture of ragtime style dance music for the masked ball and more sentimental songs for the overhearing scenes and musical interludes. The music slowed for Beatrice and Benedick's exchange during the masked ball, for example, and fairy lights gave an atmosphere of romance even though their words contradicted it. Balthasar's 'Sigh No More Ladies' in Act II, scene iii was a stag-type celebration with champagne, accompanied by a dance from Don Pedro, Claudio and Leonato. Hero and Ursula sang the 1884 sentimental 'Love's Old Sweet Song' by James Molloy and J. Clifton Binghamton to push their romantic message home to the hidden Beatrice. Its chorus 'though the heart be weary, sad the day and long, / Still to us at twilight comes love's old, sweet song' tuned in to Beatrice's barely disguised longing for love and the wider feeling of a world soon to be lost. Act III scene iv ended with strains of 'Here comes the Bride' which were ironically repeated at the beginning of the wedding scene as Don John ceremonially opened the doors of the church to reveal a procession of couples bedecked with wedding flowers. Victory bouquets had been presented to Don Pedro at his first entrance, though in later scenes roses became much more heavily weighted tropes of romance. Claudio's epitaph was cut and replaced by a wreath of white and pink roses to commemorate Hero. Leonato sadly left Hero's bouquet on the front pew before exiting in IV.i. He and Antonio drowned their sorrows with copious glasses of whisky in V.i, thus giving an explanation to their vehement challenges to Don Pedro and Claudio. Shakespeare was explicitly co-opted as part of the conservative, complacent establishment. Having accepted Leonato's offer of a cigar and glass of whisky, Dogberry toasted a bust of the Bard in Leonato's study.

The outside settings took up Roosevelt's pursuits as a hunter and naturalist in the domesticated environment of Leonato's garden with its ornamental pond. Hunting was, of course, a common trope of courtly love poetry and lines like Don Pedro's 'What need the bridge much broader than the flood' (I.i.297), spoken from a wooden bridge, effectively literalised the hunting metaphors of courtship. Don John's failure as a social animal or a man of action was neatly conveyed when he tried and failed to shoot one of Leonato's ducks. Benedick began Act II scene iii in a canoe, choosing to fish rather than love. When Don Pedro and Leonato stalked him, he comically transformed himself into a not-very-convincing fish by lying down in the hull and laboriously paddling towards them while Claudio remarked 'this fish will bite' (II.iii.110).

A portrait of Roosevelt above the judge's seat in the courthouse was quickly reversed to reveal Dogberry's own portrait and self-important authority. Dogberry (Barnard Hughes), Verges (Will Mackenzie) and the Watch were presented as the Keystone Cops by costumes, accompanying piano music, and allusions to the original silent films of 1912–17. The film shifted to black-and-white footage as Seacoal made the precarious climb onto the penthouse to witness Borachio's conference with Conrade. A childish 'tower of hands' gag in the style of Laurel and Hardy in IV.ii effectively made the long arm of the law part of the film's appeal to spectators' nostalgia for the America of the past. In Act V scene i. Dogberry congratulated himself on being recognised as a 'shallow fool' who brought matters to light by giving his partner Verges a handshake. As well as being very funny, the moment highlighted the dangers of complacency.

The film was not simply nostalgic. Reflections in the water and in mirrors showed characters thinking about their place. Don Pedro and Claudio gazed down from a bridge to the water before plunging into romance, while Benedick looked at his reflection on 'I did not think I should live till I were married' (II.iii.224–5). Such moments also asked viewers to reflect on what they were seeing. In addition to showing Hero's teddy bear, the production dwelt on a model carousel, displayed on the fireplace in Leonato's house, as if to warn viewers of the dangers of watching the film, or their own past, with naïve, rose-coloured spectacles. At the end of V.i, after Leonato and Antonio had heard Borachio's confession and set up the second-wedding plot, they also set in motion the model wooden carousel. The scene ended with a close-up on this toy playing its childish, sweet music. Full sized hand-carved merry-go-rounds numbered between 5000 and 6000 in the early decades of the 1900s, and, as Gaiman's novel *American Gods* suggests, are icons of an American golden age of success (Gaiman, 2001). Reducing the icon to a domestic ornament, perhaps even a toy belonging formerly to Hero, suggested the fragility of the domestic scenes of security and harmony presented in the film. The reappearance of Hero among the masked ladies for the resurrection scene built on the effect. They entered to the music of the model astride white horses on a life-size toy carousel, wearing white dresses and veils and thus presenting an idealised image of self-conscious nostalgia. The carousel looked beautiful, absolutely artificial and naively childish, as an approach to marriage or to life.

Insecurities about masculine identity were bound up with the film's self-conscious nostalgia. Leonato (Mark Hammer) was a kindly father rather than a dominant patriarch; the whole of his diatribe against

Hero in the wedding scene was cut and the character's anachronism, as part of a bygone age, was emphasised. Filming Benedick (Sam Waterston) and Claudio (Glenn Walken) taking baths in the barracks as they discussed their impressions of Hero (I.i.154–83) exposed their vulnerability once out of uniform. Cigar smoking was a dominant trope for masculinity (as in the 1990 RSC production), but although the soldiers gave the appearance of fitting easily into their peacetime costumes, the emergence of female agency in their absence was hinted at from the opening scene when Beatrice (Kathleen Widdoes) challenged the messenger and Benedick's military prowess. She concluded their first parry of wit by taking his pint glass and drinking his beer. Benedick's complaint that every word of Beatrice's tongue 'stabs' was a rare moment of direct address to the camera.

Men were unsure how to interact with women in this environment, which reflected the emergence of first-wave feminism in the 1900s and spoke to a generation of men trying to find their place between the action of the Vietnam war and second-wave feminism at home. Don Pedro (Douglass Watson) epitomised the difficulties they faced in a social no-man's land where traditional codes of romance were no longer reliable. Don Pedro was unable to recognise that Beatrice's gift of a rose for his buttonhole was a piece of business to cover her sense of hurt at having 'lost the heart of Captain Benedick' (II.i.254) and went on to propose seriously to her. After a lengthy pause, he went on one knee to ask 'Will you have me, lady?' only to be rejected as a joke. A close-up showed him looking out over a large bunch of roses, nearly in tears, and at his brave words 'we are the only love-gods' (II.i.357) he smelt the rose Beatrice had given him. His sense of hurt carried over to the overhearing scene where the line 'I would she had bestowed this dotage on me' (II.iii.165) was addressed direct to camera. His wish that Benedick 'would modestly examine himself to see how much he is unworthy so good a lady' (II.iii.201–2) was spoken with a hint of bitterness, straight to the canoe where Benedick was hiding.

Benedick's traditionally romantic approach to Beatrice was also precarious. She threw his bunch of roses to the floor when he told her nothing but foul words had passed between him and Claudio, only later accepting the tokens of romance by picking up the flowers, sharing glasses of champagne and kissing him on the balcony. Beatrice and Benedick's relationship offered a microcosm of the cultural uncertainty in a period of transition between traditional and

modern modes of gender relations. In Act III scene ii Hero and Ursula
literally poured cold water over Beatrice's more aggressive feminist
sensibilities by turning on a sprinkler at the spot where she was hiding
in the conservatory. Nevertheless, even when Beatrice and Benedick
were tricked into romance, they both continued to behave unconven-
tionally. The small screen was especially effective in conveying this.
It exaggerated the vehemence of their aggressive words and gestures
within the heavily decorated domestic surroundings, juxtaposing
this with moments of soft focus and slow motion to mark the lure
of traditional romance. Although the film offered a fairy-tale ending
with only Don Pedro as a quietly marginalised figure, the dangers
of believing in that world were highlighted by the repetition of
soft-focus images from the wedding scene which had been so easily
directed and disrupted by Don John. The film presented its idealised,
old-style American Messina as no less fragile than a dream inspired
by an expensive childhood toy.

BBC Television Shakespeare (1984)

Much Ado About Nothing was the play Cedric Messina chose to pilot
the BBC TV series of Shakespeare's Complete Works, but the initial
production – starring Michael York as Benedick, Penelope Keith as
Beatrice and Arthur Lowe as Dogberry (1978) – was never publicly
broadcast. The British Film Institute holds an incomplete copy, running up to the end of Act III scene iii, which reveals some of the
problems encountered in this early experiment, in spite of a promising
cast and some good performances by Keith and York. The set was
much too small to allow adequate freedom of movement for the
actors or the imagination. Leonato's household was suggested by a
sunken terrace surrounded by wooden steps, walls and a pagoda-like
structure. Overcrowding rather than overhearing was a recurrent
hazard. By contrast, the costumes were much too large and extravagant in scale for television. Finally, although Arthur Lowe was well
known for his role as the pompous Captain Mainwaring in the popular
television series *Dad's Army*, for some reason he failed to capture the
comedy of Dogberry.

The play was reattempted at the end of the series in 1984, directed
by Stuart Burge and starring Robert Lindsay as Benedick and Cherie

Lunghi (who had played a forceful Hero in Barton's 1976 production) as Beatrice. The beautiful design drew on lessons from earlier productions in the series: Elijah Moshinsky's effective use of Vermeer-like interiors for his painterly production of *All's Well*, and Jane Howell's deliberately artificial children's playground for the *Henry VI* plays. The sets (by Jan Spoczynski) suggested that Leonato's house and gardens were extensive: a large courtyard set dominated by a lion statue and surrounded by colonnaded walks from which characters watched each other in a series of middle-distance shots; an inner hall with a large staircase down which the diners and maskers entered to dance in the ball scene; a series of inner rooms and archways. It was easy to believe that the church ceremony, attended only by members of the household, took place in Leonato's private chapel.

If, as Gary Waller has argued, television's appeal is at least partly due to its peculiar ability to 'create an intimacy between two rooms, ours and that of the screen' (1988, 23), the sets were unlikely to appeal to most viewers on this level. Their overdetermined historicism suggested a romanticised, former age. Presenting a place of privilege and wealth gave substance to the production's reading of Claudio (Robert Reynolds) as a fortune hunter. All the characters except for Don John's group were costumed in rich brocades: the older characters in brown and gold and the younger generation in warm shades of red and pink. The women's dresses were Italian, early 16th-century fashion, with Beatrice looking remarkably like Bartolomeo Veneto's painting of Beatrice D'Este, the Duchess of Milan (held in the Snite Museum, University of Notre Dame), whose wedding gown is described by Margaret in Act III scene iv. The beginning of that scene showed Hero choosing a ferronière (a jewel worn on the forehead, on a cord or chain), an accessory she wore throughout, that signalled her identity as a 'jewel' to be bought by Claudio (I.i.171).

The masked ball, with elegant dances accompanied by atmospheric early music, offered a sumptuous display of colour and made it easy to see how even Jon Finch's very camp Don Pedro could be seduced by romance in this wealthy home. As Don Pedro retreated under an archway with Hero and Leonato, mid-shot, Claudio's suspicion (in close-up) did not seem unfounded, though it was more difficult to tell whether his sense of loss extended beyond Hero's wealth to her person. He seemed so surprised by his good fortune at having won her hand, which she confirmed with a nod, that one sensed little affection between them. Reynolds's Claudio was a beautiful, self-assured and rather vain young man, but not so youthful as to excuse his behaviour. His rejection of Hero in the chapel was motivated by hurt pride rather than love. His joking with Don Pedro in Act V scene i indicated no sense of remorse, even when he learned of Hero's death. The mourning scene was another elaborate show: a decorous procession of figures in black cloaks and white masks offered a *memento mori* with candles and a solemn hymn during which Claudio showed little emotion. The restoration of Hero was the remaking of an ostensibly good bargain with the wealthy Leonato. Don Pedro's enjoyment of showy matchmaking, in suggesting that Benedick was not 'the unhopefullest husband' for Beatrice (II.i.348–9), was simultaneously a matter of negotiation with her wealthy guardian. In this production Don Pedro had no personal interest in her; his proposal was a comic performance made from behind his mask.

The spectacular environment explained Beatrice and Benedick's need to perform. In Act I scene i, Beatrice emerged artfully from behind a pillar to reprimand Benedick for still talking, and she dominated the relationship throughout. Benedick, obviously fascinated by her, observed (in close-up) how much she exceeded Hero, and was unable to take his eyes off her as she stood with her cousin and uncle, mid-shot, at the opposite side of the courtyard. Cherie Lunghi made good use of Beatrice's skirt to flounce decorously away from 'the prince's jester' during the dance, leaving Benedick wounded by her wit. Lindsay's attempts to laugh off the experience were not convincing and he protested too much about wanting to be sent to the world's end by Don Pedro. Beatrice's stillness always gave her higher status. Lindsay's Benedick was not at ease; his laughter often betrayed nervousness, he was unsure where to put himself and found it difficult to maintain eye contact with the camera or anyone else for more than a few seconds. His lack of self-confidence, in spite of his bravado, made him a much more sympathetic figure than Claudio.

Don Pedro and Don John's plots were bound to succeed in a household with numerous colonnades, balconies, doorways and gateways. The walled orchard opened out from the courtyard and, in spite of the presence of real oranges (eaten by Benedick and used as bowls by his boy in II.iii), it was obviously artificial. The pictorial style, evoking scenes from a book of hours, followed what John Wilders regarded as the most satisfactory way directors had found to televise Shakespeare because 'it calls attention to the artifice of the plays' (Wilders, 1981, 13). It was highly appropriate for the staged overhearing episodes. These were filmed from several angles but in most cases keeping both eavesdropper and plotters together in shot in order to maximise the full comic effect. A hint of tension between Beatrice and Hero was suggested when the former held a flower against the side of the bower and Hero, offering to devise slanders to 'empoison' Benedick's liking, vigorously plucked it.

The light and colour of these open scenes, presided over by Finch's festive, artful Don Pedro, was set against much darker, inner rooms occupied by Don John. According to Robert Lindsay, Burge, as director, had wanted the play's 'dark centre to be there all the time' (Lindsay, 1984) and this was personified by Vernon Dobtcheff's Don John. Looking like a malevolent version of Rembrandt's St Paul, he brooded quietly amidst heavy, oak furniture, his elegant velvet costume suggesting wealth and power equal to Leonato's. In spite of his self-declared villainy, there was no anger, just a cool, leisurely malice as he finished his glass of wine and smiled at the thought of mischief. His bribery of Borachio, dressed likewise in black with black hair, formed a dark counterpoint to the negotiations between Leonato and Claudio. During the church scene, Don John's black figure literally shadowed Don Pedro and when they next appeared both Don Pedro and Claudio had changed into expensive black costume as though indicating his influence. Benedick donned black in Act III scene ii as a melancholy lover, and by Act V scene i it looked as though Don John's style would take over. Antonio's determination to challenge Claudio was ridiculous; Don Pedro and Claudio's arrogance was disturbing. Their callous jokes made it very difficult for Benedick to keep his promise to Beatrice and issue his challenge. Darkness culminated in the monument scene, before which Beatrice and Benedick could do no more than exchange nervous jokes. When Ursula appeared with the good news, they quickly broke off their developing intimacy and their kiss was postponed until the final scene.

The pivotal exchange between Beatrice and Benedick in the church was curiously downplayed in this production. Everyone was embarrassed by what had happened: not only Claudio's behaviour but that of Leonato (played skilfully by Lee Montague). Hero's faith in herself and the Friar's optimism that 'this wedding day / Perhaps is but prolonged' (IV.i.253–4) made the atmosphere intensely awkward rather than tragic. The stiff formality of everyone's conduct, before and after the event, arguably alienated viewers from the world of the play. Beatrice and Benedick's low-key human contact helped to restore the connection by creating a surprising moment of 'intimacy between two rooms', that of the action and those of the viewers (Waller, 1988, 23). As Beatrice sat on the floor, Benedick handed her his clean handkerchief and she unthinkingly returned her wet one to him. Having tucked it away, he sat down next to her on the floor. This was where the demand to 'Kill Claudio' was made. Lindsay played Benedick's relations with Claudio and the Prince as tenuous to begin with, so there was no extensive struggle of loyalty for him in the brief exchange which followed.

Robert Lindsay was a household name to British viewers and the production pursued this tactic for familiarisation by casting Michael Elphick and Clive Dunn as Dogberry and Verges. Both these actors were well known to television audiences from their appearance in popular comedies and advertisements, though Elphick had also played Shakespearean roles at the Royal Court and on Broadway, experience which showed in his expert handling of Dogberry's prose. Casting these two as the outsiders who stumble, with extreme self-confidence, from a dusty gaol into Shakespeare's language and the elite glamour of Leonato's house, offered a comic paradigm of viewers' own experiences. Arguably, in this production, Dogberry and Verges were not just a means to resolve the plot or the providers of comic relief. They were television everymen whose homely presence in the world of Shakespeare's Messina provided an easy point of access to an environment which for many viewers was visually and verbally alien.

The final scene returned to a public environment of domestic festivity, perhaps one with which the original television audience could still make connections since *Much Ado* was broadcast during the Christmas season. Beatrice and Benedick were on their guard again with Beatrice rather cruelly scoring an extra point by getting all the ladies to laugh with her at Benedick on 'No more than reason' (V.iv.74). Their kiss removed any doubt about their feelings, contrasting with the more tentative expressions of affection between Hero and Claudio. As appropriate for a television version, the production ended with a celebration of inclusive domestic opulence rather than romance, as everyone danced in couples around Leonato, the master of the household.

Romantic tourism in Kenneth Branagh's
Much Ado About Nothing (1993)

The film of *Much Ado About Nothing* directed by Kenneth Branagh and starring him and Emma Thompson has achieved wide popularity and attracted critical interest, more for its treatments of gender and romance than for its cinematic techniques. As Michael Hattaway observed, somewhat surprisingly this film makes very little use of the camera as voyeur to explore questions of perception or critically interrogate the nature of the gaze, issues that would seem highly appropriate to the play's concerns with watching and being watched (1998). The film does make clever use of point of view to explore Branagh / Benedick's relationship with Beatrice and the camera, but for the most part its favourite technique seems to be the long, panning shot, as in the opening which sweeps the beautiful countryside and the picnic; in Act II scene iii which captures the languorous heat and leisure of the summer scene around the fountain; or in the final shots where the camera is craned up to look down on happy figures dancing in and out of the villa and gardens. Such camera work creates an illusion of inclusive romance that is entirely in keeping with the director's aims to present a 'film for the world', a popular Shakespeare in which 'audiences [could] react to the story as if it were in the here and now and important to them' and 'to be as international as possible' (Branagh, 1993, x). The film's popularity and box-office success attests to the accuracy of Iain Johnsone's view that it is 'life-affirming and full of fun and positively contagious when it comes to the enviable opiate of smitten love' (*Sunday Times*, 29 August 1993).

What makes it immediately engaging is the film's opening live shot depicting a villa amidst luscious Tuscan countryside, a prospect enjoyed by members of Leonato's household as they relax in the sun, laughing and eating fruit. This idyllic scene is packaged as Shakespearean tourism by two other elements in the opening. The film begins with the cinematic equivalent of a prologue by projecting the first words of Balthasar's song onto a black screen as they are spoken by Emma Thompson, accompanied by guitar, then full orchestral score as the scene opens to reveal first Leonato's painting of his house and then the 'real' Italian scenery. As Thompson continues reading the lyric, with its references to 'one foot in sea and one on shore' warning of men's deceit 'since summer first was leafy', spectators are inducted into a world of holiday romance. Shakespeare is utopian escape, a journey to an exotic destination advertised by Leonato's painting but much better in the flesh, as is coyly suggested when the camera pans across from the bodies of those picnicking to Emma Thompson's bare foot and suntanned legs and then up to her smiling face as everyone joins in with the final chorus line 'Hey nonny nonny'. Scenes of anticipated sexual excitement dominate the next pre-title sequences which show the soldiers in leather trousers galloping forward on horseback (à la *Magnificent Seven*) and Leonato's household rushing back to the villa, both groups then casting off their clothes and throwing themselves into baths to wash and dress for the formal meeting. This is shot from above to show the protagonists from each group set opposite each other in the shape of a large X or kiss. Branagh's strategy of cutting over 40 per cent of the lines in favour of cinematic image make the film itself something of a holiday from the text.

The atmosphere of holiday romance works extremely well for the masked ball. Like a destination nightclub, its exotic excitement provides the ideal context for raucous flirting (in older and younger characters) and confusion. Thompson's Beatrice enjoys the carnivalesque opportunities it gives to 'know and not know' the Benedick who puts on a silly foreign accent as well as his mask (II.i.186–7), while Claudio's readiness to believe that 'friendship is constant in all other things / Save in the office and affairs of love' (II.i.159–60) is a familiar story of holiday romance to the audience of tourists who have plunged into the Tuscan environment evoked so powerfully by the film's use of music and colour.

The film deliberately softens its portrayal of Claudio (Robert Sean Leonard) and plays up the youthful romanticism between him and Hero (Kate Beckinsale). Leonato gives a knowing smile to Hero at the latter's mention of Claudio. Hero looks down in regret in response to her father's sympathetic, almost apologetic wish that she accept the Prince's courtship in Act II scene i (his prior knowledge of Don Pedro's intentions can only be the result of the opening greeting since I.ii is cut). Most importantly, the film provides a credible reason for Claudio's behaviour by showing Margaret and Borachio having sex at the window in which Claudio had previously spotted Hero looking down at him, Juliet-like. This meeting is referred to obliquely in the text; in the film, a close-up on Claudio's face engages the audience's sympathy with a shattering of innocence. The wedding scene demonstrates his brutality, but the cutting of most of his lines makes this appear far less calculated. Leonard's Claudio pushes Hero over a bench and furiously pulls down all the wedding decorations, his rage making him seem more immature than malicious. The casting of Claudio becomes increasingly important as the main plot veers towards tragedy, since it recalls Leonard's previous performance in the film *Dead Poets Society* (1989) and, Sam Crowl argues, appeals to 'a particularly American sentimentality about the precariousness of youthful innocence' (Crowl, 2002, 121). The camera spends several minutes following a lengthy mourning procession, which is shown to Hero from a window above, and Claudio breaks down at the door of the tomb in floods of tears. The film's final scene plays out the tragicomic rewriting of *Romeo and Juliet* with full sentimental aplomb: the couple are reunited in tears of joy.

Benedick and Beatrice's closeness to Claudio and Hero and their plight was motivated by identification in Branagh's film. He explained 'Emma Thompson and I both wanted to suggest former lovers who had been genuinely hurt by their first encounter which perhaps occurred at the tender age of Hero and Claudio in the play' (Branagh, 1993, xi). Beatrice's opening quotation that 'Men are deceivers ever' functioned as a subtle but nonetheless resonant hint of a pre-play history in which Benedick had won her heart with false dice. Thompson's performance showed the hurt Beatrice still felt with an economy of tone and gesture that suggested depth. In their opening encounter the buzz of chatter fell silent at 'Scratching could not make it worse' (I.i.130), making their argument suddenly very public. As Benedick broke it off, Thompson's Beatrice retorted 'You always end with a jade's trick' and then quietly completed the line herself with the words 'I know you of old' and a sad look to the camera (I.i.139–40). She was embarrassed by her error in prompting a proposal from Don Pedro, another moment that revealed something beyond her apparently 'merry heart'. It was not as easy to see what, if anything, lay behind Benedick's obvious irritation at romance and his own lack of success in it. His impatience with – and embarrassment about – sexuality was clear when he hesitated in protesting he should never 'hang my … bugle in an invisible baldrick' and get married (I.i.226–7).

Although these lovers were more mature than Hero and Claudio, their developing relationship was no less emotionally magnetic. Benedick's difficulties in managing his deckchair at one side of the hedge in the overhearing scene was matched by a deliberate overplaying of the script-within-the-script by Don Pedro, Claudio and Leonato. They sat in a line at the edge of the fountain enjoying their group-identity as mischievous 'lads', using their hands to mime a bird and explain Benedick's equally ridiculous ploy to cover his shout of excitement with a birdcall. Both Beatrice and Benedick showed their delight at having a second chance in love by making an escapist return to youthful activities. The camera intercut shots of Benedick throwing his hands in the air for joy and exuberantly splashing through the fountain with images of Beatrice playing on a swing for sheer pleasure and excitement. Sam Crowl compares the marriage between Beatrice and Benedick to that the film makes between Shakespeare and Hollywood, and draws attention to parallels between the understanding Beatrice and Benedick reach and the '"equality of consciousness between a man and a woman" that [the director Stanley] Cavell uncovers at the center of his Hollywood comedies'. Crowl perceptively analyses Branagh's direction of Act IV, scene i, when they enter the chapel, pointing out that we first see Beatrice, kneeling by the altar, from Benedick's perspective and that '[t]hey aren't squared to the camera because they aren't yet square with each other'. Beatrice's passionate denunciation of Claudio transforms Benedick and '[f]or the first time in the film Branagh allows Benedick to look directly into the camera's eye as he determinedly confronts his emotional commitment to Beatrice'. As he determines to engage himself to challenge Claudio, Crowl argues that '[h]ere he steadies and fixes his gaze because to engage the camera is to engage Beatrice' (Crowl, 2002, 119).

Emma Thompson's Beatrice thus occupies a central position in the film. Constantly associated with fruit, which she eats or feeds to others – even the incoming messenger – she is a conduit for the film's emotional energy: the pleasures and sufferings of characters and spectators.

As its prologue suggests, the film is a female-centred tour of Shakespearean romance, perhaps designed to appeal primarily to female spectators in its promotion of sentimental youthful romance, its stark representation of brutality at the wrecked wedding, its narrative of reforming the hero, and its image of sexual equality.

In spite of such a politically correct, popular appeal to women, this point of entry promotes a dominantly heterosexual guide to Shakespearean romance. In a brilliant analysis that takes as its starting point the iconic black leather trousers worn by Don John (played by

Keanu Reeves) and his men, Celestino Deleyto shows how the film advertises 'the pressure of homoerotic desire' on the generic structure of romantic comedy and on 'a social structure based on heterosexuality' (Deleyto, 1997, 92). By casting sex symbol Reeves as the villain Don John, the film immediately casts other forms of sexuality into the 'underground' world of the cellars beneath Leonato's villa and simultaneously calls into question such prejudice. Hero looks at her hand with some concern after Don John kisses it in passing, but Act I scene ii shows Reeves's beautiful torso being massaged by Conrad and displayed in front of a fire. The film substitutes homosexuality for the early modern stigma of illegitimacy and displays it via Reeves's enunciation of Don John's line 'I cannot hide what I am' (I.ii.12). The film's great difficulty in separating its 'conscious critique of patriarchal male bonding from a more ambivalent, but at times very powerful homophobia' (Deleyto, 1997, 99) is figured in the exclusion of Don Pedro, whose intermediary position is signalled by his costume of blue leather trousers. (To follow this visual metaphor through, Thompson's Beatrice, our guide to the film, wears the shortest skirt, perhaps suggesting her role as a campaigner for women's equality.) The jollity of the heterosexual wedding dance at the end of the film is chillingly disturbed by the return of Don John to the screen, who looks knowingly across at his half-brother. Neither participates in the dance or reappears on the screen.

The casting of Denzel Washington means that Don Pedro's isolation, featured in so many performances, is inflected by racial difference as well. Although the camera loves Washington, he is doubly 'othered' in the film by the actor's black skin and the character's position as head of a military unit that fosters exclusively male bonding. Leonato and Antonio, played by the veteran British actors Richard Briers and Brian Blessed, are the companionable heads of the cosy family group in the villa. Through their close bonding, shown often by affectionate physical embraces, the film figures a protective, non-threatening side to patriarchy. Leonato's shocking rejection of his daughter (following Don Pedro and Don John's lead) shows the dangers of abuse inherent in his dominant position. In spite of Don Pedro's gracious attempts to integrate himself into the family through his proxy wooing, matchmaking and proposal to Beatrice, he is unacceptable. The film's collapse of gender politics and homophobia has the unfortunate additional effect of excluding this black man from its white wedding dance. As Courtney Lehmann argues, for all Branagh's claims to make a Shakespeare film 'for the world', this *Much Ado* is also 'a fairy tale of class harmony which builds its castles in the sand of racial antagonism' (1998, 16). (Even more ignorant, in performance terms, is the cod Irish accent and misplaced casting of comedian Ben Elton as Dogberry.) Cultural tourism into the idyllic Italian landscape of Shakespearean romance via Branagh's film is much more dangerous than it appears.

6   Critical Assessment

The 18th century

Much Ado's early editorial and performance history laid the foundations of a critical tradition that prioritised the Beatrice–Benedick plot. Charles Gildon, writing a commentary to Rowe's edition of 1709, disliked the generic instability of the play, arguing that although it must be called a comedy it contained improbable "incidents" of 'a tragic strain' that would never 'have come off in nature' without a full tragic conclusion. The gulling of Don Pedro and Claudio was 'lame' and the plot was only effective because 'the character of Don John the Bastard is admirably distinguished', meaning consistently defined in terms of 'a sour, melancholy, saturnine, envious, selfish, malicious temper – manners necessary to produce these villainous events' (quoted in Bloom and Cornelius, 2010, 52). Claudio's accusation of Hero on such 'weak grounds without farther examination' made it 'highly contrary to the very nature of love' and so unconvincing as well as being unnatural in its effect: 'too shocking for either Tragedy or Comedy'. The tragic strain was only redeemed, in Gildon's view, by Leonato's passion. The play's tragicomic cocktail of effects did not attract critical appreciation until the 20th century. To sensibilities at the dawn of the enlightenment, it was the integrity and distinction of characters 'perfectly maintain'd' which allowed readers and audiences to 'lose the absurdities of conduct in the excellence of the manners, sentiments, diction'. These appeared most admirably in 'all that passes betwixt Benedick and Beatrice' in Gildon's view. While praising their wit and loquaciousness, he was careful to note differences between the equally talkative rake Lucio in *Measure for Measure* and Benedick, 'a gentleman and a man of spirit and wit'. Both the overhearing scenes were, he felt, managed 'with that nicety and address that we are very well pleas'd with the success, and think it very reasonable and just' (Furness, 1899, 347).

Mrs Elizabeth Griffith, daughter of the manager of the Theatre Royal, Dublin, and an actor herself, expressed a different view of the overhearing scenes in her *Morality of Shakespeare's Plays Illustrated* (1775). While recognising that Hero's critique of Beatrice's 'most unamiable character of pride and self-conceit' did fall 'properly within the moral tendency of these notes to expose to view', Griffith referred to slandering another person as 'a wicked device' (153–54). She went on to remark it was 'so very irksome a theme, that it disgusts me to dwell upon it' (155). Nevertheless, it served as a useful platform from which to commend Beatrice's passionate attack on the falsehood of men, and to make a wider feminist point. 'There is a generous warmth of indignation in this speech which must certainly impress a female reader with the same sentiments upon such an occasion', Griffith pointed out. Its naturalness answered 'the design of my introducing it, which is, to vindicate my sex from the general, but unjust charge of being prone to slander', that is, slandering others. Beatrice's vehement objections to Claudio were justified since 'there is nothing which a woman of virtue feels herself more offended at than defamation' and the scene proved that the vice was 'neither masculine, nor feminine; *tis the common of two*' (159, Griffith's emphasis). Griffith pursued her condemnation of Claudio rather than Beatrice more explicitly in her notes on Act V scene i where she commended the justice of Antonio's contempt for 'the bragging profligates of those or, indeed, of any times' (161).

Elizabeth Inchbald, who had also acted Shakespeare professionally and was part of the theatrical circle of John Philip Kemble and Sarah Siddons, likewise disapproved of the 'pitiful act of private overhearing' which the play staged. Its shortcomings were mitigated only by Beatrice and Benedick whose 'highly entertaining' quality was matched with respectability since 'they are so witty, so jocund, so free from care, and yet so sensible of care in others'. Don John was a cause of further social impropriety because of his illegitimacy. Inchbald noted, somewhat mischievously, 'Shakespeare has given such an odious character of the bastard, John, in this play, and of the bastard, Edmund, in *King Lear*, that, had these dramas been written in the time of Charles the Second, the author must have been suspected of disaffection to half the court' (Furness, 1899, 348). Charlotte Lennox gave broad consideration to the play but limited her comments on Dogberry and the Watch by defining them as 'Two or three absolute Ideots' without 'the least Ray of Reason to direct them' (quoted in

Bloom and Cornelius, 2010, 60). William Hazlitt went even further than this, wryly observing that

> Dogberry and Verges in this play are inimitable specimens of quaint blundering and misprisons of meaning; and are a standing record of that formal gravity of pretension and total want of common understanding, which Shakespeare no doubt copied from real life, and which in the course of two hundred years appear to have ascended from the lowest to the highest offices in the state.

> (Hazlitt quoted in Furness, 1899, 348)

Whatever the rules of social decorum which purportedly dictated responses to the play at the turn of the 19th century, Hazlitt's comments convey delight in the play's anarchic and nonsensical elements.

The 19th century

Through the 19th century, women played an increasingly significant part in shaping prevailing opinions of the play both as the subject of critical interest and as writers and performers. In addition to commentaries on Shakespeare's women by Anna Jameson (published in 20 editions from 1832–1905), Mary Cowden Clarke (1850–52) and Henrietta Palmer (1859), actors such as Fanny Kemble (1868), Helena Faucit (1885) and Ellen Terry discussed the roles in print or in lectures. Critics and theatre producers alike found difficulty in fitting Beatrice into the idealised model of 19th-century femininity, which was perhaps one reason behind a slow shift to redress the balance and pay attention to the Hero–Claudio plot as well. Maria Foote's Beatrice 'of the drawing room,' who was 'oily, gentle and tender, and lady-like' in Kemble's 1829 production was one extreme, while editor Thomas Campbell (1838) thought Beatrice's assertive behaviour made her an 'odious woman' (Cox, 1997, 22–23). Anna Jameson observed, somewhat reprovingly, that Beatrice's character, 'being taken from general nature, belongs to every age'. Having criticised Beatrice as a 'termagent', she went on to openly acknowledge the double cultural standard which made Benedick 'by far the most pleasing' of the two 'because the independence and gay manner of indifference of temper, the laughing defiance of love and marriage, the satirical freedom of expression are more becoming to the masculine than to the feminine character'.

At the same time she praised Beatrice's exuberance of feeling and her 'energy of spirit' as having significantly more emotional depth than the heroines of modern comedy. Such a combination of morally admirable and socially reprehensible traits was challenging, Jameson acknowledged. It 'required a profound knowledge of women to bring such a character within the pale of our sympathy' (Jameson, 2005, 111–12).

The difficulties Beatrice posed are perhaps best exemplified by Ellen Terry's experience of the role. Even by the latter part of the century, she had to steer a delicate line in playing a Beatrice 'more feminine and delicate than Shakespeare intended' and 'reconstructed on a nineteenth-century plan' (*Boston Daily Advertiser*, 28 February 1884, cited in Cox, 1997, 41). At the same time, she pointed out tellingly, 'Women who have fought the heart breaking battle against prejudice in any age do not need to be told what it is that "kills" Beatrice' in Act IV scene i of the play (Cox, 1997, 42).

Henrietta Palmer's ideal portraits of womanhood in *The Stratford Gallery; or the Shakespeare Sisterhood* (1859) found only one virtue in Beatrice: saving the present generation 'by proving in her own person that the "fast" woman is by no means a modern "institution"'. Palmer condemned the character for being 'the slave of a pert tongue' whose intellect 'though quick, is not strong enough to keep her vanity in subjection'. Although nature made her 'a spirited, generous, clever woman', her usual affectation meant that her wit was 'but the dazzle of words', far inferior to the sympathy of Rosalind in *As You Like It*: 'the two compare as the cold artificial glitter of a diamond with the cordial warmth of sunshine'. Palmer saw no integrity in Beatrice's love for Benedick which she dismissed as 'an experimental freak'. For Palmer, Beatrice had just two redeeming moments. Her soliloquy at the end of Act III scene i (where, of course she reflects on her reputation for pride and scorn) was deemed 'creditable alike to her heart and her good sense', while her vigorous defence of Hero in the church helped to redeem her 'gratuitous impertinence and unseemly forwardness'. Hero, by contrast, was lauded for her delicacy, and Palmer criticised the play's construction in affording Beatrice the place of leading lady 'not the first time, by the by, that loud and persistent vanity has succeeded in usurping the honorable place belonging to modest, graceful excellence' (Palmer quoted in Thompson and Roberts, 1997, 111–12).

Opinion about the two heroines shifted markedly by the end of the century. The professionalisation of Shakespeare criticism in the New

Shakespeare Society, founded in 1874, gave Grace Latham the authority to write against the 19th-century tradition of applauding more submissive models of femininity in Shakespeare. Her essay on Hero (1891) pointed out that 'discipline has been an exterior tyranny, not the lesson of self-government', and used Hero's fate to make a trenchant critique of Victorian social education as dangerous, a cause of potential tragedy:

> Obedience and submission are duties to her, and have been instilled into her until they have become an instinctive habit. Gentle, modest and unassuming, she plays her part in society, with a quietness which is only saved from insipidity by its grace and good breeding. This short, brown creature is the ideal young lady of parents and teachers, and in truth she is as perfect as her education will allow her to be … But alas! Hero has lost any small power of self-assertion, or of independent action that she may ever have had. She can only open her lips when there is no fear of contradiction; a slave does not tell her desires lest they should be thwarted.
>
> (Latham quoted in Thompson and Roberts, 1997, 171)

Latham's conception of slavery at the end of the century is strikingly different to that of Palmer, writing at the height of Victorian celebrations of the angel in the house.

An emerging sense of *Much Ado*'s place in the Shakespearean corpus, inspired by Edward Dowden's campaign to study Shakespeare's mind and art, informed Frederick Furnivall's Introduction in *The Leopold Shakespeare* (1877). In addition to discussing the Beatrice and Benedick plot as a more sophisticated development of the taming process in *Shrew*, Furnivall paid attention to Dogberry and Verges, comparing their relationship to that of Bottom and his companions; their linguistic infelicities to scenes in *Merry Wives*; and their interactions with Leonato to those between the Gobbos and Bassanio in *Merchant of Venice*. Most perceptively, Furnivall read the Hero–Claudio plot as a prototype for more mature craftsmanship in *The Winter's Tale*, a comparison that has been developed by 20th century critics (Furnivall, 1877, liv–lvi).

Twentieth-century and recent criticism

Swinburne's view that no Shakespearean play could compare with *Much Ado* for 'absolute power of composition, for faultless balance and blameless rectitude of design' was eccentric in the 19th century and remained so at the beginning of the 20th. Modernist attempts to find a unifying pattern to the play were more prominent in Craig and Jackson's theatre designs than in criticism (see pp. 114–116). The problem of finding tonal coherence can be seen in a 1926 volume entitled *Shakespeare's Heroines*, with illustrations of possible stagings by Charles Ricketts. Compiled by Lilian Baylis, Frank Benson and Edith Evans to raise money for a new Shakespeare Memorial Theatre, the book was a record of Sunday afternoon broadcasts given by 'distinguished actresses and actors'. Baylis described Shakespeare's heroines as 'extraordinarily modern', but Beatrice exemplified the problems presented by the whole play. 'We never see her in repose', the article complained, noting that in spite of her intelligence and 'assured bearing in polite society' she was 'curiously immature'. Her lack of experience of 'life in its less pleasant aspect' became obvious from her impetuous and imperious behaviour in the church scene, and her return to her 'old tricks' at the end of the play suggested to the authors that she had not learnt anything. Perhaps impatience with Beatrice as 'provocative, brilliant, delightful' said more about the critics' dislike of teasing inconsistencies in the play. It may have appeared trivial in a period following loss in the First World War (Baylis 1926).

Plots, sources, intertexts

Consideration of the play's sources, many of which had been quoted in Furness's Variorum edition, was revived with the publication of Charles Prouty's full-length study *The Sources of Much Ado About Nothing* in 1950. Among other illuminating analyses of the changes made to character and plot line by Shakespeare, Prouty put forward a forceful though not altogether persuasive defence of Claudio as a young man following the proper conventions of early modern courtship and arranged marriage. Subsequent critical work has reconsidered the double-plot structure, drawn attention to further intertexts for the play, and taken up consideration of *Much Ado*'s generic hybridity. D. Cook (1981) reconsiders the play's interwoven plots and its curious juxtaposition of tragic and comic moods. Marta Straznicky (1994) discusses the generic tensions in the play while Mihoko Suzuki (2000) examines gender and class as factors that complicate the ideology of comic form.

John Traugott (1982) analyses what the genres of comedy and traditional romance as found in the play's sources bring to the play. Martin
Mueller (1994) examines 'Shakespeare's sleeping beauties', the use of a
female character who dies and (sometimes) comes back to life, which
derives from Bandello's story of Timbreo and Fenicia. The motif is found
in *Much Ado About Nothing* and repeated with a range of variations in the
figures of Juliet, Desdemona, Cordelia, Imogen and Hermione, Mueller
shows. Melinda Gough (1999) discusses Shakespeare's play alongside
epic romance and anti-theatricality, focusing on Hero as a version of
the beautiful enchantress exposed as a whorish hag, a type found in
Spenser's *Faerie Queene* and deriving from Ariosto's tale of Ariodante
and Ginevra and from the classical figure of Circe. Gough argues
that Claudio's shaming of Hero can be read as 'not only Shakespeare's
critique of epic-romance violence but his implicit response to contemporary attacks against the stage' (44). Specifically Italian intertexts have
been explored by Laurie E. Osbourne (1990) in a study of weddings
in novellas, and by Philip Collington (2006) who makes a persuasive
case for reading Castiglione's *The Book of the Courtier*, translated by Sir
Thomas Hoby in 1561, as informing the play of manners in *Much Ado*.

Much ado about signifying

William G. McCollum proposed that '*Much Ado* is very popular with
audiences but somewhat less so with critics' (1968, 165), because it
appeared to lack the serious exploration of love found in other comedies.
John Russell Brown (1957) put forward an alternative view, arguing
that it set forward 'Shakespeare's ideas about love's truth' and 'the
need for our imaginative response to it' in order to realise distinctions
between inward and outward beauty (109). Even though A.P. Rossiter
(1961) claimed that '*Much Ado* is not a "serious" play', he allied it with
a group of 'problem plays' and identified a fruitful topic for future
research by suggesting that 'misapprehensions, misprisons, misun-
derstandings, misinterpretations and misapplications are the best
names for what the play is "about"' (77). R.G. White pointed out the
pun on the play's title – 'nothing' and 'noting' being pronounced alike
in Shakespeare's day, thus giving the title significance since 'all the
personages are constantly engaged in noting or watching each other'
(Furness, 1899, 6). The idea of deception in the play was discussed by

Richard Henze (1971) and Barbara Lewalski (1968), the latter pointing out connections between the masquerade in the ball scene, the gulling of Beatrice and Benedick, and the play acting of Margaret as Hero as dramatic negotiations with Renaissance neoplatonic discourses on love. Nova Myhill (1999) gives a perceptive analysis of how the play's staging of spectatorship self-consciously manipulates and educates its own audiences about the ways they watch.

James McPeek's inspiring reading of the thief 'Deformed' (1960) considers the importance of fashion in contemporary satires in order to present the personification in *Much Ado* as an 'inverse craftsman', a fictional embodiment of the insights, deceptions and self-deceptions which the play dramatises. McPeek argues that, 'as a gentleman Deformed has social license to continue his career of deception: appearance so often coincides with reality that people are habitually led into trusting appearances' (1960, 65, 74). David Lucking (1997) takes the post-structuralist implications of McPeek's article further to argue that *Much Ado* 'continues to insist on the precariousness of the relation between sign and meaning' (8) because Deformed is, in some sense, 'the presiding genius of the play, no less present for being absent' (23). Dawson (1982) gives further insights into the play or 'much ado' that is made of discursive practices. Stephen Dobranski's close reading of the play's imagery of sex, pregnancy and loss argues that these fragments evoke the illusion of a past sexual relationship between Beatrice and Benedick. The potentially tragic element of the Hero–Claudio plot 'represents the present displacement of Beatrice and Benedick's earlier romance' by furtively suggesting their pain (1998, 245).

The play's preoccupation with language and error is personified by Dogberry, whose role John Allen analyses in a magnificently penetrating and witty article (1973). Dogberry is funny because he combines 'the air and mannerisms of a veritable sage with utterances and behavior so inane as to produce a splendidly bathetic contrast' (36). As the 'nonpareil of beatific self-appreciation', however, he embodies the self-regarding tendencies of other characters in the play, most obviously the villain Don John but also the 'cheerful egoists' Beatrice and Benedick and the self-righteous Leonato. Claudio and Don Pedro's sense of honour is akin to Dogberry's, Allen argues, and even Hero demonstrates a 'genteel complacency'. Dogberry is, then, to the manor born in Messina; 'a comic everyman as egoist', he is 'the gross exemplar of an attitude which is endemic there' (37). Dogberry's confidence in his superior wisdom and blindness to self-knowledge hints at similar shortcomings in Don Pedro and in Claudio at the end of the play. Allen shows how Dogberry is, albeit inadvertently, responsible for illuminating truths via his malapropisms and 'speaking some of the lines that lie at the satiric heart of *Much Ado*' (46). His view that 'a thief will soon show himself what he is and steal out of your company' is shared by the Friar, who is confident that Hero will be exonerated (48). Allen suggests, rather surprisingly, that Dogberry bears comparison to more noble figures like Prospero or Duke Vincentio in *Measure for Measure* since he functions as 'a special kind of *deus ex machina*' (38). His tendency to mercy rather than revenge obliquely critiques Beatrice's desire to eat Claudio's heart in the market place (50) and stands as a reminder of the tolerance for human faults that is required if tragedy is to be avoided. Dogberry is not the only figure to be remembered as an ass for pomposity and mistaking. The audience's delight in the character is all the more powerful since the play invites our indulgence 'not only for Dogberry himself but for the Dogberry-like qualities of other characters in the play and even, by extension, in ourselves' (39).

Language, wit and wisdom

The ways in which *Much Ado* plays with linguistic and literary forms has been taken up by several critics including Barish (1974), who considers the pattern and purpose in its extensive use of prose, and Hunt (2000) who looks at how the plot enacts a reclamation of language. Lynne Magnusson (1999) analyses the play's reiteration of everyday speech forms and how speech deforms and repairs social relations, paying attention to Dogberry as a dramatisation of how 'politeness and policing' intersect (161). In discussions of the play's games with language and form, its references to sonnets have been neglected until recently but Patrick Cheney gives a beautifully nuanced reading of *Much Ado* as 'a discourse of and a fiction about sonneteering and theater' (2007, 363). Cheney analyses the lyrics of Balthasar's song as words that are opposed by Don Pedro's matchmaking project and Benedick's 'failed sonneteering' in Act V scene ii (368). The defamation of Hero as a false book, and the intensity of the epitaph and the 'solemn hymn' to Diana as 'a haunting space' marks a change in attitude on the part of the men (377). In the final moments of the play when sonnets are produced to prove Beatrice and Benedick's love for each other, Shakespeare dramatises a shift from theatre to poetry and validates 'the art of the sonnet as an important cultural institution for individual identity and social relationships' (379).

Critics in the 20th and 21st century have revisited the play's sparkling display of 'wit' that had proved so attractive to 18th-century commentators. William G. McCollum (1968) reads it as a rhetorical strategy that depends on tension for its effect, linking it to the mix of comic and tragic effects in the play. '*Much Ado* is not only like wit; it can be seen as a witticism in tripartite form – the joke, of course, is on Claudio' (173), he argues. Carl Dennis's essay 'Wit and Wisdom in *Much Ado*' proposes that the play stages an opposition of 'wit', which relies on the pragmatic assessment of sensory evidence, and 'belief', which characters learn to live and love by. In a striking reversal of 18th-century attitudes, Dennis here defines wit as bad since it depends on scepticism and leads to isolation. Instead, the play prioritises genuine love which 'entails giving up the outer eye of reason for the inner eye of faith' (Dennis, 1973, 229).

Ian Munro (2004) introduces a class perspective to the ways wit is perceived in the play, analysing how the courtly, improvisational wit practised by Beatrice and Benedick is set against the marketplace wit of the jestbook *A Hundred Merry Tales*, which it stigmatises as the product of cheap print. Noting that the play was probably the farewell performance of Will Kemp, he argues that 'if the noble characters are anxious about their courtly self-fashioning, the play itself is anxiously appropriating this courtly façade as part of its own strategy of cultural advancement' (91). The play's apparent privileging of courtly wit is perpetuated through editorial practice, but Munro takes a different approach to consider the jestbook as 'an example of the burgeoning publication of wit' in early modern England. Printed jest books often conflated the sexual and textual, particularly through jests relating to cuckoldry, an example of female wit that informs the play's sexual jokes.

Individuals, social interaction and gender

Because of its setting in Messina, *Much Ado* did not fall into the major group of 'festive comedies' analysed so powerfully by C.L. Barber, and did not fit easily into the 'green worlds' of comedy discussed by Northrop Frye. Following the lead set by L.C. Knights's historicist study in *Drama and Society in the Age of Jonson* (1937), however, good analyses of the social dynamics dramatised in the play have been published. These drew timely attention to the roles of Don Pedro and Don John which had been relatively neglected in earlier critical writing. James Smith's early essay on deception (1946) regarded the two plots as intertwined with each other and the social world of Messina. Steven Rose (1970) identified a disturbingly powerful element of self-love as well as love in the protagonists' speech. Michael Taylor (1973) went further, arguing that the self-interest of the protagonists, especially Benedick and Beatrice, constituted a danger to the social order since their antipathy to marriage pointed to a world which would not be peopled. Barbara Everett analysed the play as an 'unsociable comedy' (1994). Elliot Krieger's essay, 'Social Relations and the Social Order in *Much Ado About Nothing*', which appeared in a volume of *Shakespeare Survey* (1979) dedicated to the play, gave a close anatomy of the social tensions that fuelled Don John's plots. *Much Ado* is, he argues, 'an inquisition into the values of a society that refuses to question its values', the 'clearest dramatic treatment' of the difficulties faced by a ruling class that attempts to mask the traditions and appearances that underlie its elitism. Drakakis (1987) focuses on the ideological construction of Don John as a bastard to demonstrate how the discursive practices of Messina and early modern England work in the service of patriarchal ideology in order to 'ensure the placing of individual subjects in relation to a state apparatus, one which masks, but would by no means exclude the exploitation of one class by another' (1987, 73). The importance of honour in Messina, the high stakes in maintaining social status and the ways that the tragicomic plot dramatises processes of public shaming and redemption are explored in studies by Fernie (2002), Findlay (2010) and Chamberlain (2009). One distinctive strand of historicist criticism has analysed the fast-changing fashion at the end of the 16th century as a crucial intertext for understanding social interaction in the play. Articles by David Omerod (1972) and Michael Friedman (1993) pay attention to sartorial imagery and metaphor and to stage costume, while other commentaries on the play (e.g. McPeek, 1960; Allen, 1973; Cook, 1986; Findlay, 2003) consider fashion as one of the discursive modes employed in the play's examination of status and gender.

The issues of gender difference which had preoccupied 19th-century critics so frequently were brought to the fore again by Barbara Everett's seminal analysis of *Much Ado* as a play in which 'the woman's world dominates' (Everett, 1961). It was this, she argued, which had made the play less popular as the subject of critical writing. Conversely, with the rise of feminist criticism, *Much Ado* became the object of extensive study. A wide range of readings by men and women, too numerous to list individually, followed. The pioneering volume *The Woman's Part: Feminist Criticism of Shakespeare* included two essays focusing on *Much Ado*. Carol McEwin considered Act III scene iv where Hero, Margaret and Beatrice meet on the wedding morning as an example of intimate conversations between women in Shakespeare's plays. Janice Hays focused on Hero and the sexual distrust of women that is incubated in the traditionally male sphere of war. Woman's role is to 'lead the male protagonist away from the individualistic aspiration, assertiveness and narrow fictionality that characterise the male role in Renaissance society' (Hays, 1980, 79). Michael Friedman (1993) considered the silencing of Beatrice and Hero as part of their preparation to become wives. Cook (1986) noted the persistent preoccupation with cuckoldry in the play and argued that Beatrice, for all her assertive independence, 'tacitly accepts her culture's devaluation of "feminine" characteristics of weakness, dependence, vulnerability'. Carol Thomas Neely (1993) gave a definitive reading of how the play's 'tensions and its poise are achieved by the interactions of the two plots' revolving around the climax of the broken nuptial. Jean Howard (1994) analysed how the play's numerous staged shows, masquerades, interior dramatists and actors, are representations of theatrical practice that self-consciously produce and reproduce differences of gender and class.

The performance of gender in *Much Ado* has been explored from a theatrical perspective too. Penny Gay (1994) devoted a chapter of *As She Likes It* to productions from 1949 to 1990. The actor Maggie Steed, who played Beatrice in Di Trevis's 1988 RSC production, discusses the tyranny of being the family entertainer that Beatrice seems to experience since 'the role she has found for herself is that of the clown – still the outsider, "singing for her supper"' (Steed, 1993, 45). Sinead Cusack explained how she brought out 'other areas of the character' besides the femininity for which she had been cast in Terry Hands's 1982 production. 'A Beatrice who gets very angry.

A woman who has been damaged by society' (Rutter, 1988, xvi). In comparing the roles of Beatrice and Katherina, the actor Janis Stevens commented: 'one of the big challenges of the role is that she not become the shrew ... It's an action she plays' (44). Stevens outlined Beatrice's position in 'a very superficial world of a cornered market on femininity, a cornered market on masculinity' which come together in 'party-oriented moments of time when everybody has a great time, but nothing real actually happens' until the proposal from Don Pedro, which Beatrice has to weigh carefully and think through (Stevens, 2007, 41–42).

In Stevens's performance, the spontaneous demand to 'Kill Claudio' was motivated partly by a sense of exclusion from the soldiers' community: 'She understands this male bonding that he is so much a part of and she, I am sure, despises it in some ways as women are often more jealous of their man's male friends than they ever would be of another woman because that kind of camaraderie is very difficult for a woman to compete with' (Stevens 2007, 50–51). In contrast, female bonding with Hero was a substitute for Beatrice's lack of success in loving Benedick: 'I have been preparing her to be this absolute, perfect young lady who is going to find the perfect love. And if I can't have it in my own life, then, by golly, I'm going to make sure that my little girl has it' (46). Liz Schafer's *Ms-Directing Shakespeare* discusses productions of *Much Ado* directed by Gale Edwards (Adelaide, 1987), Di Trevis (RSC, 1988), and, most usefully, gives a detailed account of Helena Kaut-Howson's production at the Royal Exchange Theatre in Manchester in 1997. The latter was particularly notable for its staging of Act III scene iv with Hero having a bath which 'created a sense of women's space; open, relaxed but also fragile' and its presentation of Don John as 'passionately obsessed with Claudio' (Schafer, 2000, 83–85).

Harry Berger's essay on sexual and family politics (1982) drew attention to the power of male bonding in the play. 'The Men's Club of Messina', he argues, follows in a long cultural tradition of all-male communities sustained by an 'apprehensive reliance on power', an 'excessive attachment to *machismo*' and 'fear of love and women' (310). Both Hero and Don John fall victims to the dominant ideology. 'The play's two scapegoats are a bastard named Trouble and a woman named Hero' and Don John is a product of it, 'a testimony both to his father's prowess and his mother's sin – a by-product of the frailty named Woman' (311). Richard A. Levin's *Love and Society* in *Shakespearean Comedy* (1985) reads the play as a very dark comedy and focuses useful attention on Claudio as a mercenary wooer and Don Pedro as the head of an all-male community of soldiers. Don Pedro's sense of isolation is discussed in terms of repressed reluctance to surrender the all-male community, possibly motivated by homosexual desires for Claudio. Celestino Deleyto (1997) pursues this line of enquiry in an analysis of Kenneth Branagh's film (*see above* pp. 142–143). With detailed reference to the play, he discusses how the film deals 'at length with the threat that homosexual desire may pose to the central heterosexual romance' (1997, 2) and how it explores gender relationships in the genre of romantic comedy represented by Shakespeare's text.

Further Reading

Editions

Foakes, R.A. and Stanley Wells (eds), *Much Ado About Nothing* (Harmondsworth: Penguin, 1968).

Furness, H.H. (ed.), *Much Ado About Nothing*, Variorum edition (London: Lippincott, 1899).

Mares, F.H. (ed.), *Much Ado About Nothing*, New Cambridge Shakespeare (Cambridge: Cambridge University Press, 1988).

McEachern, Claire (ed.), *Much Ado About Nothing*, Arden Third Series (London: Cengage Learning, 2005).

Zitner, S.P. (ed.), *Much Ado About Nothing*, Oxford Shakespeare (Oxford: Oxford University Press, 1993).

Text and early stage history

Armin, Robert, *The Italian Tailor and His Boy by Robert Armin, Servant to the Kings most excellent Maiestie* (London: Robert Triphook, 1609).

D'Avenant, Sir William, *The Law Against Lovers* in *The Works of Sir William Davenant* Vol. II (London: Henry Herringman, 1673), pp. 272–329.

Digges, Leonard (ed.), *Poems: Written by Wil. Shake-speare. Gent.* (London: Thomas Cotes, 1640).

Galey, Alan. 'Dizzying the Arithmetic of Memory: Shakespearean Source Documents as Text, Image, and Code', *Early Modern Literary Studies* 9.3, Special Issue 12 (January, 2004): 4.1–28 <URL: http://purl.oclc.org/emls/09-3/galedizz.htm>.

Greg, W.W., *The Shakespeare First Folio: The Text and Its Bibliographical History* (Oxford: Oxford University Press, 1955).

Malone Society, *Collections* Vol. VI (Oxford: Oxford University Press, 1962) [Lord Treasurers' Accounts of court performances].

Miller, James, *The Universal Passion* (1737) (London: Cornmarket Editions, 1969).

Murphy, Andrew, *Shakespeare in Print: A History and Chronology of Shakespeare Publishing* (Cambridge: Cambridge University Press, 2003).

Wells, Stanley, 'Editorial Treatment of Foul-Paper Texts: *Much Ado About Nothing* as a Test Case', *Review Of English Studies* 31 (1980), pp. 1–16.

Sources

Ariosto, Ludovico, *Orlando Furioso in English Heroical Verse*, trans. John Harington (London: Richard Field, 1591).

Bandello, Matteo, *La Prima Parte De Le Novelle Del Bandello* (Lucca, 1554), Novella XXII, translated by Geoffrey Bullough in *Narrative and Dramatic Sources of Shakespeare: Volume II, The Comedies 1597–1603* (London: Routledge, 1958), pp. 112–134.

Mueller, Martin, 'Shakespeare's Sleeping Beauties: The Sources of *Much Ado About Nothing* and the Play of their Repetitions', *Modern Philology* 1: 3 (1994), pp. 288–311.

Osbourne, Laurie E., 'Dramatic Play in *Much Ado About Nothing*: Wedding in the Italian Novellas and English Comedy', *Philological Quarterly* 2 (1990), pp. 167–188.

Prouty, Charles, *The Sources of Much Ado About Nothing* (New Haven: Yale University Press, 1950).

Traugott, John, 'Creating a Rational Rinaldo: A Study in the Mixture of the Genres of Comedy and Romance in *Much Ado About Nothing*', *Genre* 15 (1982), pp. 157–181.

Intellectual and cultural context

Albott, Robert (ed.), *Englands Parnassus: or the choysest flowers of our moderne poets* (London: N. Ling, C. Burby and T. Hayes, 1600).

Anon, *Jane Anger, Her Protection for Women: To defend them against the Scandalous Reportes of a late Surfeting Lover, and all other like venereans that complaine so to bee overcloyed with womens kindnesse* (London: Richard Jones and Thomas Orwin, 1589).

Arbeau, Thoinot, *Orchesographie* (1589), trans. Mary Stewart Evans with introduction and notes by Julia Sutton (New York: Dover Publications, 1967).

Brissenden, Alan, *Shakespeare and the Dance* (London: Macmillan, 1981).

Harrison, William, 'Chapter 7 Of their Apparell and Attire' Description of England in Raphael Holinshed, *Chronicles*, second edition (London: John Harrison, George Bishop, Rafe Newberie and Thomas Woodcocke, 1587).

Lyly, John, *The Anatomy of Wit* (London: Gabriel Cawood, 1578).

Marston, John, *The Scourge of Villainie* (London: James Roberts, 1598).

Middleton, Thomas, *Collected Works* (ed.), Gary Taylor and John Lavagnino (Oxford: Clarendon Press, 2007).

Montagut, Barthélemy de, *Louange De La Danse* (ed.), B. Ravelhofer (Cambridge: Renaissance Texts from Manuscript, 2000).

Nashe, Thomas, *Christ's Teares over Jerusalem* (London: Andrew Wise, 1598).

Norden, John, *The Mirror of Honour* (London: Thomas Man, 1597).

Ian Payne, *The Almain in Britain c. 1549–1675 A Dance Manual from Manuscript Sources* (Aldershot: Ashgate, 2003).

Smith, Henry, *A Preparative to Marriage* (London: Thomas Man, 1591).

Stubbes, Philip, *The Anatomie of Abuses, Part II* (London: William Wright, 1583).

Seng, Peter J., *The Vocal Songs in the Plays of Shakespeare: A Critical History* (Harvard: Harvard University Press, 1967).

Varchi, Bernadetto, *The Blazon of Jealousie* (London: John Busbie, 1615).

Productions of the play on stage and screen analysed

Alexander, Bill, dir. *Much Ado About Nothing*, Royal Shakespeare Company, 1990. Prompt book RSC/SM/1/1990/MC2, The Shakespeare Centre Library, Shakespeare Birthplace Trust.

Antoon, A.J., (dir.) and Joseph Papp (producer), *Much Ado About Nothing*, CBS Television, 1972.

Branagh, K., dir. (and actor), *William Shakespeare's Much Ado About Nothing*, Samuel Goldwyn Company, Renaissance Film Production, 1993.

Burge, Stuart (dir.) and Shaun Sutton (producer), *Much Ado About Nothing*, BBCTV / Time Life Production, 1984.

Cooke, Antony (dir. for BBCTV), *Much Ado About Nothing*, based on the National Theatre Production, 1965–67, BBCTV, 1967, British Film Institute.

Henkel, Karin, dir. *Viel Lärm Um Nichts* Schauspielhaus, Zurich, November 2010.

Jackson, Sir Barry, (producer and actor) and Conal O'Riordan (dir.), *Much Ado About Nothing*, Birmingham Repertory Theatre, May 1919, revived May 1920, promptbook Birmingham Repertory Theatre Archive, Birmingham Central Library.

Messina, Cedric, dir. *Much Ado About Nothing*, unbroadcast production, BBCTV, 1978. Copy of Act I scene i-Act III scene iii British Film Institute, London.

Zeffirelli, Franco, dir. *Much Ado About Nothing*, National Theatre, Old Vic. London, 1965–67, Prompt Books RNT/SM/1/14 and RNT/SM/1/14a/ reports RNT/SM2/1/11 programme RNT/PP/1/1/53 Royal National Theatre Archives, National Theatre Studio, London.

The play in production, performance and on film

Branagh, Kenneth, *Much Ado About Nothing by William Shakespeare: Screenplay, Introduction and Notes on the Making of the Movie by Kenneth Branagh* (New York: W.W. Norton & Co., 1993).

Cochrane, Claire, *Shakespeare and the Birmingham Repertory Theatre 1913–1929* (London: Society for Theatre Research, 1993).

Cox, John F., *Much Ado About Nothing: Shakespeare In Production* (Cambridge: Cambridge University Press, 1997).

Crowl, Samuel, 'The Marriage of Shakespeare and Hollywood: Kenneth Branagh's *Much Ado About Nothing*,' in Courtney Lehmann and Lisa S. Starks (eds), *Spectacular Shakespeare: Critical Theory and Popular Cinema* (Cranbury: Associated University Presses, 2002), pp. 110–24.

Deleyto, Celestino, 'Men in Leather: Kenneth Branagh's *Much Ado About Nothing* and Romantic Comedy', *Cinema Journal* 36: 3 (1997), pp. 91–105.

Fitzgerald, Percy, *Henry Irving: A Record of Twenty Years at the Lyceum* (London: Chapman and Hall, 1893).

Furnivall, F.J., 'Introduction' to *The Leopold Shakespeare* (London: Cassell and Company Ltd., 1877).

Gaiman, Neil, *American Gods* (London: Headline Books, 2001).

Gay, Penny, *As She Likes It: Shakespeare's Unruly Women* (London: Routledge, 1994).

Holland, Peter, *English Shakespeares: Shakespeare on the English Stage in the 1990s* (Cambridge: Cambridge University Press, 1997).

Hattaway, Michael, '"I've processed my guilt": Shakespeare, Branagh and the Movies', in J. Bate, J.L. Levenson and D. Mehl (eds), *Shakespeare and the Twentieth Century* (Newark: University of Delaware Press, 1998), pp. 194–211.

Jackson, Sir Barry, 'Costume', in George Sheringham and R. Boyd Morrison (eds), *Robes of Thespis* (London: Ernest Benn Limited, 1928), pp. 65–72.

——'Producing the Comedies', *Shakespeare Survey* 8 (1955), pp. 74–80.

Leeper, Janet, *Gordon Craig: Designs for the Theatre* (Harmondsworth: Penguin Books, 1948).

Lehmann, Courtney, '*Much Ado About Nothing?* Shakespeare, Branagh, and the "nation popular" in the Age of Multinational Capital', *Textual Practice* 12 (1998), pp. 1–22.

Lindsay, Robert, Interview with Henry Fenwick, *Radio Times*, 22 December 1984.

Loney, Glenn, 'Review: Theatre Abroad: Oh to Be In England: A London Theatre Album', *Educational Theatre Journal*, 19: 1 (1967), pp. 87–95.

Mason, Pamela, *Text and Performance, Much Ado About Nothing* (Manchester: Manchester University Press, 1992).

'Plays Produced at Birmingham Repertory Theatre From 10th February, 1919, to 26 June, 1920' (pamphlet), Birmingham Repertory Theatre Archive, Birmingham Central Library.

Nicholls, David, *Shakespeare Retold, Much Ado About Nothing*, dir. Brian Percival (BBC 2005).

Roosevelt, Theodore D., *The Rough Riders* (New York: Charles Scribner's Sons, 1899).

Rutter, Carol (ed.), *Clamorous Voices: Shakespeare's Women Today* (London: Women's Press, 1988).

Scrapbook of cuttings and programmes, 1917–20 Birmingham Repertory Theatre Archive, Birmingham Central Library.

Steed, Maggie, 'Beatrice', in Russell Jackson and Robert Smallwood (eds), *Players of Shakespeare 3* (Cambridge: Cambridge University Press, 1993), pp. 42–51.

Stevens, Janis, Interview with H. R. Coursen, in Michael W. Shurgot (ed.), *North American Players of Shakespeare: A Book of Interviews* (Cranbury: Associated University Presses, 2007), pp. 37–53.

Waller, Gary F., 'Decentering the Bard: The BBC-TV Shakespeare and Some Implications for Criticism and Teaching', in James Bulman and H.C. Coursen (eds), *Shakespeare on Television* (Hanover, New Hampshire, 1988), pp. 18–30.

Wilders, John, 'Adjusting the Set', *Times Higher Education Supplement*, 10 July 1981, p. 13.

Critical assessments

Allen, John F., 'Dogberry', *Shakespeare Quarterly*, 24 (1973), pp. 35–53.

Barish, Jonas A., 'Pattern and Purpose in the Prose of *Much Ado About Nothing*', *Renaissance Studies*, 60: 2 (1974), pp. 19–30.

Baylis, Lilian (ed.), *Shakespeare's Heroines* (London: Ferestone Press, 1926).

Berger, Harry Jr., 'Against the Sink-a-Pace: Sexual and Family Politics in *Much Ado About Nothing*', *Shakespeare Quarterly*, 33 (1982), pp. 302–13.

Bloom, Harold and Michael G. Cornelius (eds), *Bloom's Shakespeare Through The Ages: Much Ado About Nothing* (New York: Infobase Publishing, 2010).

Brown, John Russell, *Shakespeare and His Comedies* (London: Methuen 1957).

Chamberlain, Stephanie, 'Rotten Oranges and Other Spoiled Commodities', *Journal of the Wooden O Symposium*, 9 (2009), pp. 1–10.

Cheney, Patrick, 'Halting Sonnets: Poetry and Theater in *Much Ado About Nothing*,' in Michael D. Schoenfeldt (ed.), *A Companion to Shakespeare's Sonnets* (Oxford: Blackwell, 2007), pp. 363–382.

Collington, P.D., '"Stuffed with all honourable virtues": *Much Ado About Nothing* and *The Book of the Courtier*', *Studies in Philology*, 103: 3 (2006), pp. 281–312.

Cook, C., 'The Sign and Semblance of Her Honour: Reading Gender Difference in *Much Ado About Nothing*,' *PMLA*, 101 (1986), pp. 186–202.

Cook, D., 'The Very Temple Of Delight: The Twin Plots of *Much Ado About Nothing*', in Antony Coleman and Antony Hammond (eds), *Poetry and Drama 1570–1700: Essays in Honour of Harold F. Brooks* (1981), pp. 32–46.

Dawson, Antony, 'Much ado about Signifying', *Studies in English Literature*, 22:2 (1982), pp. 211–221.

Deleyto, Celestino, 'Men in Leather: Kenneth Branagh's *Much Ado About Nothing* and Romantic Comedy', *Cinema Journal*, 36: 3 (1997), pp. 91–105.

Dennis, Carl, 'Wit and Wisdom in *Much Ado About Nothing*', *Studies in English Literature*, 13: 2 (1973), pp. 223–237.

Dobranski, Stephen B., 'Children of the Mind: Miscarried Narratives in *Much Ado about Nothing*', *Studies in English Literature*, 38: 2 (1998), pp. 233–250.

Drakakis, John, 'Trust and Transgression: The Discursive Practices of *Much Ado About Nothing*', in Richard Machin and Christopher Norris (eds), *Post-Structuralist Readings of Poetry* (Cambridge: Cambridge University Press, 1987), pp. 59–84.

Everett, Barbara, '*Much Ado About Nothing*,' *Critical Quarterly*, 3 (1961), pp. 319–335.

——'*Much Ado About Nothing*: The Unsociable Comedy', in M. Cordner, P. Holland and J. Kerrigan (eds), *English Comedy* (Cambridge: Cambridge University Press 1994), pp. 186–202.

Fernie, Ewan, *Shame in Shakespeare* (New York and London: Routledge, 2002).

Findlay, Alison, '*Much Ado About Nothing*', in Jean E. Howard and Richard Dutton (eds), *The Blackwell Companion to Shakespeare: The Comedies* (Blackwell Publishers, April 2003), pp. 393–410.

——'Surface Tensions: Ceremony and Shame in *Much Ado About Nothing*,' *Shakespeare Survey*, 63 Peter Holland (ed.) (2010), pp. 282–90.

Friedman, Michael D., '"For man is a giddy thing, and this is my conclusion": Fashion and *Much Ado about Nothing*', *Text and Performance Quarterly*, 13 (1993), pp. 267–282.

——'Hush'd on Purpose to Grace Harmony: Wives and Silence in *Much Ado About Nothing*', *Theater Journal*, 42: 3 (1990), pp. 350–363.

Howard, Jean E., *The Stage and Social Struggle in Early Modern England* (London and New York: Routledge, 1994).

Gough, Melinda J., '"Her Filthy Feature Open Showne" in Ariosto, Spenser and *Much Ado About Nothing*,' *Studies in English Literature*, 39: 1 (1999), pp. 41–67.

Griffith, Mrs [Elizabeth], *The Morality of Shakespeare's Drama Illustrated* (London: Cadell, 1775).

Hays, J., 'Those "soft and delicate desires": *Much Ado* and the Distrust of Women', in Carolyn Ruth Swift Lenz, Gayle Greene and Carol Thomas Neely (eds), *The Woman's Part: Feminist Criticism of Shakespeare* (Urbana: University of Illinois Press, 1980), pp. 79–99.

Henze, Richard, 'Deception in *Much Ado about Nothing*', *Studies in English Literature*, 11: 2 (1971), pp. 187–201.

Hunt, Maruice, 'The Reclamation of Language in *Much Ado About Nothing*', *Studies in Philology*, 97 (2000), pp. 165–191.

Jameson, Anna Murphy, *Shakespeare's Heroines* (ed.), Cheri L. Larsen Hockley (Peterborough: Broadview, 2005).

Knights, L. C., *Drama and Society in the Age of Jonson* (London: Chatto, 1937)

Krieger, Elliott, 'Social Relations and the Social Order in *Much Ado About Nothing*', *Shakespeare Survey*, 32 (1979), pp. 49–61.

Levin, Richard A., *Love and Society in Shakespearean Comedy: A Study of Dramatic Form and Content* (Newark: University of Delaware Press, 1985).

Lewalski, B., 'Love, Appearance and Reality: *Much Ado* About Something', *Studies in English Literature*, 8 (1968), pp. 235–251.

Lucking, D., 'Bringing Deformed Forth: Engendering Meaning in *Much Ado About Nothing*', *Renaissance Forum*, 2:1 (1997), http://www.hull.ac.uk/renforum/v2no1/lucking.htm.

Magnusson, Lynne, *Shakespeare and Social Dialogue: Dramatic Language & Social Dialogue* (Cambridge: Cambridge University Press, 1999), pp. 153–162.

McCollum, William G., 'The Role of Wit in *Much Ado About Nothing*', *Shakespeare Quarterly*, 19 (1968), pp. 165–174.

McKewin, C., 'Counsels of Gall and Grace: Intimate Conversations between Women in Shakespeare's Plays', in Lenz, Greene and Neely (eds), *The Woman's Part* (Urbana: University of Illinois Press, 1980), pp. 117–132.

McPeek, James A., 'The Thief "Deformed" and Much Ado about "Noting"', *Boston University Studies in English*, IV (1960), pp. 65–84.

Munro, Ian, 'Shakespeare's Jestbook: Wit, Print, Performance', *English Literary History*, 71 (2004), pp. 89–113.

Myhill, N., 'Spectatorship in/of *Much Ado About Nothing*', *Studies in English Literature*, 39: 2 (1999), pp. 291–312.

Neely, Carol Thomas, *Broken Nuptials in Shakespeare's Plays* (New Haven: Yale University Press, 1985).

Omerod, D., 'Faith and Fashion in *Much Ado About Nothing*', *Shakespeare Survey*, 25 (1972), pp. 93–106.

Rose, Steven, 'Love and Self Love in *Much Ado About Nothing*', *Essays in Criticism*, 20 (1970), pp. 143–150.

Rossiter, A.P., *Angel With Horns* (New York: Theater Arts Books, 1961).

Smith, James, '*Much Ado About Nothing*, Notes for a Book in Preparation', *Scrutiny*, XIII, 4 (1946), pp. 242–257.

Straznicky, Marta, 'Shakespeare and the Government of Comedy: *Much Ado About Nothing*', *Shakespeare Survey*, 22 (1994), pp. 141–171.

Suzuki, Mihoko, 'Gender, Class and the Ideology of Comic Form: *Much Ado About Nothing* and *Twelfth Night*', in Dympna Callaghan (ed.), *A Feminist Companion to Shakespeare* (Oxford: Basil Blackwell, 2000), pp. 121–143.

Taylor, Michael, '*Much Ado About Nothing*: The Individual In Society', *Essays in Criticism*, 23 (1973), pp. 146–153.

Thompson, Anne and Sasha Roberts (eds), *Women Reading Shakespeare 1660–1900: An Anthology of Criticism* (Manchester: Manchester University Press, 1997).

Index